IT WILL
NEVER
HAPPEN
TO ME!

by Claudia Black, PhD, MSW

Except for the poetry, and the story "Best Little Boy In Town" names used in the book are not the true identities of the clients from which they came. Any identification is probably not mere coincidence but from the commonalities of being from an alcoholic home.

Published by
M.A.C.
Printing and Publications Division
1850 High Street
Denver, Colorado 80218

CONTENTS

Acknowledgments ....

Preface 1

Introduction. 3

Chapter 1
  Vignettes. 9

Chapter 2
  Roles. 13

Chapter 3
  Don't Talk, Don't Trust, Don't Feel. 31

Chapter 4
  The Progression of the Roles. 53

Chapter 5
  The Child Within the Home. 67

Chapter 6
  The Adult Child. 105

Chapter 7
  Family Violence. 135
    Physical Abuse
    Sexual Abuse

Chapter 8
  Resources. 155

Epilogue. 177

Appendixes. 181

ACKNOWLEDGMENTS

There are always so many people to thank after a project such as this and that is certainly true for me. In the past few years I have received a multitude of support from professional and personal friends for my work. That support has been a great motivator for me in the writing of this manuscript. While names are too numerous I would like you to know I am grateful and thank you all. Another strong motivator for me has been through the many letters I have continued to receive from young and adult children who wanted to share parts of their lives with me and expressed their thanks for clarification brought to them via my speaking seminars.

While I feel strong support from so many, there is a group of people who have been more directly involved in the creating of **IT WILL NEVER HAPPEN TO ME.** I would like to further acknowledge and thank these friends.

Martha Ranson, Vicki Danzig, Annie Doce, Bary Levy, Margaret Hillman, Lynn Sanford Tschirhart, Peter Nardi, Bob Stein for their readings and feedback.

Renee Cavalier, Joan Fiset, Jane Lesch Middleton (Juggler In a Mirror, Arthur Ward Publishers, 111 4th Avenue, Kirkland, Washington, 98033) for their poetry and Peter Nardi for his story.

Muriel Zink for her "right before publication" hours of time spent in editing and feedback.

Anne Marie Piontek for her editing.

My mother and sister for their support — support that came from their pride of me and their acceptance of my sharing myself so personally in my work.

Debbie Smith and Jael Greenleaf for their direct work with the manuscript via readings and feedback, but most of all for reminding me of the importance of this work and the importance of me taking care of me while I work.

While I have dedicated this book to Jack, I want to include him in the acknowledgments. There is no other person I am more indebted to than Jack Fahey for the fact this book exists. This book has taken nearly as much time in his life, as in mine—in hours of discussion, rewriting, feedback, motivation and patience.

Thank you all.

to Jack, whom I dearly love.

PREFACE

A 58-year old male child of an alcoholic once told me, "I spent my whole life making sure I didn't end up like my dad. And now, the only difference between my dad and me is that my dad died from his alcoholism, and I don't have to die from mine."

As I began my career in the field of alcoholism treatment, I worked predominantly with adult alcoholics who wanted to stop drinking. They were patients who had been admitted to the inpatient alcoholism treatment facility where I was employed, and where in my capacity as a social worker, I had been asked to develop a family counseling program. Consequently, I began meeting with both spouses and children of alcoholics. The children ranged in ages from 4 to 44, because by the time many alcoholics seek help, their children are well into their adulthood.

While my supervisor would have been satisfied had I counseled only spouses in my "family programming," I knew that was impossible. After all, I found over half of my alcoholic clients had been raised in alcoholic families, as were many wives of the men who were alcoholic. Every one of them had said, at some point in their lives, "It will never happen to me!"

Persons raised in alcoholic homes, who later became alcoholic themselves, had thought those same words. And, many had verbalized those words to family members and friends. Wives of alcoholic men, wives who had been raised in alcoholic homes, had repeated those identical words. In their wildest dreams, they didn't imagine it could ever happen to them. But, they married alcoholics; some even married a second, and a third alcoholic. Yet, the words, "It will never happen to me," were thought and spoken in all sincerity — those children, as adolescents and adults, honestly meant them. And, after working with the adult children, I knew, in all sincerity, their children would echo the same words.

I also knew someone had to help the children of alcoholics; I knew that knowledge of alcoholism, or being fearful of alcoholism, was not enough to stop the generational progression of the disease.

I want to acknowledge each and every one of you who have ever thought, spoken, believed, and hoped, "It will never happen to me." Because of that conviction, and because of your impact on me, maybe it never will have to happen to those children now being raised, or yet to be raised, in alcoholic families.

As well, I would like to acknowledge those who refer to themselves as "survivors." The survivors tend to be those who managed to reach adulthood without becoming an alcoholic, or marrying an alcoholic. These many adult children have patted themselves on the back for their ability to survive, and have been admired by others for this accomplishment. This book is also written with the survivors in mind because so many of them have realized they deserve more in life than just the ability to survive. They do, as we all do, deserve more. Hopefully, this book will help in that quest also.

INTRODUCTION

If you live in a typical American community, one out of six families in your neighborhood is affected by alcoholism. The effects of this disease could at sometime affect us all. Alcoholism is a disease of unknown origin, which at this writing has no known cure, though it is treatable. It's a disease which knows no distinctions; housewives, television stars, blue collar workers, professional people, clergy, physicians, astronauts and even children are stricken everyday. Only 3 to 5 percent of the alcoholic people in the U.S. are represented by the stereotypic Skid Row drinker. The so-called average alcoholic is a man or woman with family, job, and responsibilities.

The alcoholic is a person who, in his drinking, has developed a psychological dependency on the drug alcohol coupled with a physiological addiction. Alcoholics are people who have experienced a change in tolerance to alcohol and need to drink more to acquire the desired effect. They are people who neither have the ability to consistently control their drinking, nor who can predict their behavior once they start to drink. They have a need to drink which becomes progressively a greater and greater preoccupation in their lives. Alcoholics are people who, at one time in their lives, made a decision to drink just as every social drinker does. However, for them, in time drinking became not a matter of choice, but a compulsion.

Many people are confused about alcoholism because there is not one specific pattern of behavior typical to the alcoholic. Alcoholics often differ in their styles of drinking, and the consequences of their drinking vary widely. Some alcoholics drink daily; others in episodic patterns; some stay dry for long intervals between binges; some drink enormous quantities of alcohol, others do not. Some alcoholics drink only beer; some drink only wine; while for others their choice is whiskey. Still others may drink a wide variety of alcoholic beverages. Although alcoholism appears very early in the lives of some people, for others it takes years to develop. Some claim to have started drinking alcoholically from their first drink; many others report they drank for years before crossing over the "invisible line" which separates social drinking from alcoholic drinking.

In summary, alcoholics are those persons who are unable with any predictability to control their drinking, and/or whose drinking causes problems in major areas of their lives.

As people progress into the disease of alcoholism, it is most normal for the spouse to become increasingly preoccupied with the behavior of the alcoholic. This preoccupation is called co-alcoholism.

For children in the family, the combination of alcoholism and co-alcoholism results in neither parent being responsive and available on a consistent, predictable basis. Children are impacted not only by the alcoholic parent, but also by the nonalcoholic parent (if there is one), and by the abnormal family dynamics created as a consequence of alcoholism.

As different as homes are in styles of alcoholic drinking there are certain commonalities found in the effects on children. The most common consequence for children is that they are the ones, more likely than any other identifiable group, to become alcoholic. Fifty to sixty percent of all alcoholics (a low estimate) have, or had, at least one alcoholic parent. Alcoholism is a generational disease. A fact receiving more substantiation every day is that alcoholism runs in families. The exact cause of this phenomenon is as yet unknown. It is believed both genetics and the environment play a role in the onset and progression of the disease. Research indicates alcoholism may be hereditary in that there appears to be a genetic tendency toward the disease.

While children of alcoholics are at high risk to become alcoholic, research also demonstrates children of alcoholics are often prone to marry those who are, or become, alcoholic. In addition, my own research demonstrates that should a child of an alcoholic neither become alcoholic, nor marry an alcoholic, emotional and/or psychological patterns develop which may cause problems for this person in adulthood. Adult children of alcoholics often have difficulties identifying and expressing feelings. They become very rigid and controlling. Some find themselves overly dependent on others; they feel no sense of power of choice in the way they live. A pervasive sense of fear and guilt often exists in their lives. Many experience depression and frequently do not have the ability to feel close or to be intimate with another human being. These factors all play a vital role in the professional and personal lives of children of alcoholics.

If it my belief that, while science may someday determine how these children are affected biologically, we can begin to impact the role the environment plays in their lives. While children are growing up in homes affected by alcoholism, they suffer their indignities and their losses alone. . .alone because they don't perceive help and support as being available from their parents, or from other significant people.

We can become available, and we can help.

Many readers will find It Will Never Happen To Me a catalyst which provokes a multitude of feelings; many of these feelings painful. I urge you not to keep those feelings inside, but rather share them, the book will explain how to do this. For too long, family members have NOT TALKED, and have suffered in silence. Now is the time to begin the recovery process.

A person does not make a conscious choice about becoming alcoholic or co-alcoholic and, without the intrusion of alcoholism, he or she would have made other choices. So, as you read, read to understand, not to feel quilty or at blame. This book is meant to offer understanding and hope for recovery. It offers guidelines that can positively affect children of alcoholics so they can continue into adulthood with a greater sense of self, well-being, and a growing ability to have their needs met—and most importantly to live a satisfying happy life.

CHAPTER 1

Vignettes

CHAPTER ONE

I remember, as a boy, coming home from school and seeing either the living room or the dining room furniture thrown out of the drive way. It would startle me--actually it would blow my mind. My first thought would be to get it back in the house before anyone else would see it. I, or we (my mom or brothers) would get it back into the house. I would feel slightly relieved. However, for several days, or maybe a week or two, depending on the severity of the act, I would be caught up in the thought of what would happen next, such as would my dad give something of ours away to a stranger? And he did give away things we liked a lot, like a pair of skis, a rifle, and once our dog. He would tell us he hated us, or he would call us worthless so-and-so's. I would always ponder those incidents, reflecting now, I spent years worrying about dad's well being, or how I could help him. Why did he do those things? What did I do? What did we do? What could I do to make him different? I went from a young boy to a young man with my thoughts, alone, socially and mentally. I never got to know myself, and I guess I still don't. I am still a loner, I don't know how to live, to have fun or enjoy life.

Bill T., adult child-age 34

My father is an alcoholic. He has never admitted to that fact. He and my mom use to get in lots of fights when I lived at home. The six of us kids were used as pawns in their war games. I always wondered why I was causing him to drink. When the fights were going on, I always retreated to my room. There I felt secure. Now, I am 22, and have been married for two years. I have this affliction that, whenever the slightest thing happens, I always say I am so sorry. I am sorry when the milk is not cold, sorry that the wet towel was left in the gym bag. I just want to take the blame for everything, even things I have no control over.

Sharon R., adult child

I am a 29 year old woman (girl actually) who is the only child of two alcoholic parents. My parents separated when I was in 6th grade, and I continued to live with my father. When I was little, I was lonely and afraid most of the time. But when the rest of your friends seem normal and carefree, and your parents are into their own set of problems, who do you tell those things to. When I use to be awakened by my parents arguing, I longed to have a sister to talk to. Somehow I always felt if I had a sister to mother, to make things alright for, that I would have felt better. I never once thought about someone mothering me or making me feel better. I was mostly relieved when my mother left. Because at least, then, the fighting stopped. But then things kind of got turned around and I found myself being the parent and my father the child.

I prided myself on the way I was brought up because I thought it made me strong, independent and self-reliant. Now that I am older, I am so angry I feel like screaming at someone--but there is no one left to scream at. My father died in 1970 and, at that time, I guess my mother just gave up and proceeded to drink herself to death. Well, now I am almost 30 and my drinking has increased; I know it and at the same time I don't want to stop. I enjoy it, it helps me to loosen up and feel better. I started therapy last year. My therapist told me I drink to ease the pain. Maybe that is true, I never even thought about being in pain. The scary part is I seem to be emulating the very behavior and role models I shouldn't. But where do you go to undo 20 years of a life patterning style?

Barbara P., adult child

CHAPTER 2

Roles

CHAPTER TWO

There are between 28 and 34 million children and adults in America, today, who are unique. They are unique in that they are more likely than any other identifiable group to become alcoholic. They are the people who grew up, or are presently being raised, in alcoholic homes.

Why are they more likely to become alcoholic? Or marry an alcoholic? What kinds of problems do they face in adulthood as a result of their childhood experiences? What can we do to help both youngsters in alcoholic homes today, and adults who have the desire to better understand their own childhood and restructure their lives?

The following pages will help answer those questions. They are meant to help the reader understand roles children in alcoholic families adopt, and the problems they face in adulthood as a result.

While one of the clearest indicators of a smoothly working family is consistency, the words which best describe living in an alcoholic family are inconsistency and unpredictability. It is my belief that what a spouse or child does while living in an alcoholic environment, they do because at the time it makes sense to them. As the problems surrounding alcoholism cause more and more inconsistency and unpredictability in the home, the behavior of the nonalcoholic family members typically becomes an attempt to restabilize the family system. Members of this family system act and react in manners which make life easier and less painful for them.

In most well-functioning families, one finds emotions being expressed clearly, and each person being given the opportunity to share feelings. Emotions are accepted by an attentive group which offers understanding and support. Family members can freely ask for attention, and give attention to others in return.

In a home beset with alcoholism, emotions are repressed and become twisted. Emotions are often not shared, and, unfortunately when they are expressed, it is done in a judgmental manner placing blame on one another.

While constructive alliances are part of the healthy family, adult members of an alcoholic family often lack alliance. If alliances are demonstrated they are destructive and usually consist of one parent and a child (or children) against the other parent.

Families have rules which need to be verbalized, and to be fair and flexible. Rules such as "no hitting", or "everyone will have a chance to be heard," lead to healthier functioning within a system. In alcoholic family structures, should rules be established, they are usually not based on a need for healthy protection but instead are built on shame, guilt, or fear. Rather than a verbalized rule which says "there will be no hitting," there is an unspoken, silent rule which says "you won't tell others how you got that bruise."

Many times, there are clearly defined roles within the family. It is typical for adults in the family to divide, or share the roles of being the breadwinner and the administrator--the one who makes the decisions within the home. Children raised in homes where open communication is practiced and consistency of life styles is the norm usually have the ability to adopt a variety of roles, dependent on the situation. These children learn how to be responsible, how to organize, to develop realistic goals, to play, laugh, and enjoy themselves. They learn a sense of flexibility and spontaneity. They are usually taught how to be sensitive to the feelings of others, and are willing to be helpful to others. These children learn a sense of autonomy and also how to belong to a group. Children growing up in alcoholic homes seldom learn the combinations of roles which mold healthy personalities. Instead, they become locked into roles based on their perception of what they need to do to "survive" and to bring some stability to their lives.

LOOKING GOOD

   While working with adult children of alcoholics, I discovered an interesting phenomenon: in their childhood, these particular adults did not fit the stereotype of what I had been led to believe was representative of children of alcoholics. These adults were not necessarily the children who developed into runaways, who filled our juvenile justice systems, who were asthmatic or hyperactive, who performed poorly in school, or had low self-images. They weren't always the ones who had adjustment problems, nor were they always the angry ones. The majority of these people indicated, instead, that they had strong tendencies to appear "normal" and to be from "typical" American families. They did not exhibit problematic behavior, and they rarely, or never, talked about the alcoholism in their primary family.

   Should you question school counselors, workers in juvenile

justice systems and other helping professionals, they will report contact with a high percentage of children from alcoholic homes. But, that description applies more to the youngster known as the "acting out" child, and not to the majority of children in alcoholic families. I contend most children in alcoholic families are not seen by school counselors, are not addressed in juvenile justice systems, are not treated for asthma or hyperactivity. While there is a substantial number of problematic children from alcoholic homes, the majority of these children simply do not draw enough attention to themselves to even be identified as being in need of special attention. They are a neglected population. If they are busy and look good, they will be ignored.

My interest was heightened, and I began to take a closer look at these adult people raised in alcoholic homes. I was equally interested in those who became alcoholic as adults, those who married alcoholics, and those, now adults, who did neither.

In my work with young children, I found the majority of them tended to adopt one, or a combination, of the following three roles: the responsible one, the adjuster, the placater.

An only, or oldest, child, is most likely to be a very responsible child. This child not only assumes a great deal of responsibility for himself, but does so for other family members as well. This is the child who is 9-years-old going on 35, the 12-year-old going on 40. From the onset of alcoholism in the family, this child has been an adult. It is the 7-year-old putting mom to bed, the 9-year old getting dinner ready every night, the 12-year-old driving dad around because dad's too drunk to drive himself. This role is one in which the child seldom misbehaves, but rather takes on many of the household and parenting responsibilities for the other siblings and, very possibly, for the parents.

Next is the child who is usually not the oldest, or the only child, and who does not develop the need to be responsible for himself or others. The need is not as great because there is often an older sibling providing the needed structure in the environment. This middle or younger child finds the best role for him to play is that of the adjuster. It is easier to simply follow directions, handle whatever has to be handled, and adjust to the circumstances of whatever has to be handled, and adjust to the circumstances of the day. This coping pattern allows the child to appear more flexible, more spontaneous and, possibly, more selfish than others in the home.

A third common pattern of a child within this increasingly chaotic home life is that of the <u>placater,</u> the family comforter. It is this child who often tries to make others in the home feel better, as if he is responsible for whatever pain the family is experiencing. This youngster is much more sensitive to other people's feelings, and spends much time lessening the intensity of the pain within the home. The child is a good listener, taking away mom's sadness, brother's fear, sister's embarassment and dad's anger.

All of these characteristics are ones we can easily find value in and, typically, don't see as destructive. In fact, labeling children with words such as, "responsible", "caring", "ability to adjust to crisis;" allows them, as adults, to pat themselves on the back for having been such good "survivors." But, in adulthood, these ways of surviving often lead to unhealthy extremes. Such unusual development of coping behavior often results in emotional and psychological deficits. It is understanding those deficits that allows one to understand how survivors end up not surviving; but, instead, how they are drawn into problem drinking, marrying someone who becomes alcoholic, or having an unusual number of problems in their adult years.

THE RESPONSIBLE ONE

Everything must be in order in my household or it brings great anxiety to me. The orderliness probably stems from the chaos I felt in my adolescent years. My parents' house was always physically orderly, but human relationship -- wise -- CHAOS.

Children need consistency and structure. As an alcoholic progresses into alcoholism, and the co-alcoholic becomes more and more preoccupied with the alcoholic, children experience decreasing consistency and structure in the family unit, and their lives become less and less predictable. Some days, when dad is drinking, no disruption or tension occurs, but on other days when he is drinking, he becomes loud, opinionated and demanding in his expectations of the children. Mom, at times, reacts to this disrupting behavior by being passive and ignoring it; other times, she makes arrangements for the children to go to the neighbors until dad goes to bed, or tells them to go outside and play until she calls for them. The children don't know what to expect from dad when he drinks, nor do they know what to expect from mom when dad drinks.

When structure and consistency are not provided by the parents, children will find ways to provide it for themselves. The oldest child, or an only child, very often becomes the responsible one in the family. This child takes responsibility for the environmental structure in the home and provides consistency for the others. When dad starts becoming verbally abusive while drinking, this youngster gathers the coats and pajamas of the other children and heads them to the neighbor's home. While mom and dad are out drinking together the responsible one directs the other children to their bedrooms, ensures they complete their homework, instructs them to change into their nightclothes and go to bed. This is the 9-year-old girl who has a flowchart across her bedroom wall marking what she needs to do on a daily basis to take care of the house. She assumes a lot of responsibility because she feels the need for structure. In this situation, she perceives that her mother who works more than 8 hours a day is always sad and tired. Mom never complains, but this young girl knows it helps when the rugs are vacuumed, the dirty clothes ready for the laundry, the shopping completed, the dishes washed and the ironing finished. She also knows everything seems better when her brothers and sisters receive direction from her about where they can and cannot go; then they don't bother mom and dad, they do get to play, and everyone seems a lot happier.

Sometimes, the responsible children are directed to assume this role, other times, they assume the role voluntarily. One woman, age 30, said, "My mom took me out of a foster home I had been in for six years just so I could be home to take care of my two younger brothers." Another adult woman told me, "My being such a good homemaker and parent to my sister made it easier for dad to be out of the house when mom was drinking. He didn't know what to do, so he just worked later and later, and had more and more business trips." It is typical for alcoholic and co-alcoholic parents to take great pride in their adultlike youngster. The responsible child makes life easier for the parents by providing more time for the alcoholic to be preoccupied with drinking, and for the co-alcoholic to be preoccupied with the alcoholic.

Whether or not responsible children are blatantly directed into this role, or more subtly fall into it, it is typically a role which brings them comfort. Playing the responsible role provides stability in the life of this oldest, or only, child and in the lives of other family members. These responsible children feel, and are, very organized. They practice this role so consistently that they become very adept at planning and manipulating. In order to provide the structure they seek they often manipulate their brothers and sisters. This ability to organize, to effect others, to accomplish goals provides these children with leadership qualities-- qualities which get them elected as class leaders, captains of teams, etc.

Responsible youngsters become adept at setting tangible goals; i.e., 'I'll be sure the boys get their baths tonight, and the girls tomorrow night." "I'll be sure I get the grocery list done tonight, and do the shopping tomorrow after school." These goals are realistic and attainable. In an alcoholic home, one is most realistic if one thinks of goals on a short-range basis. "What can I get done today?" "What will I get done tomorrow?" If these children begin thinking about what they want to accomplish in terms of the next few weeks, or months, they know that their home situation may not remain stable enough for them to follow through with their plans. Too many long-range plans are affected by whether or not the alcoholic parent is drinking. "I never planned a birthday party for myself. If I wanted a party, the best way to have one was to call mom on my noon-hour and ask her then. It always depended on dad's mood, and she could only predict it a few hours ahead." So, in setting goals and making them realistic enough to be accomplished, the child feels good about himself. He achieves the goals and he experiences a sense of accomplishment.

Thus, responsibility, organization, setting and achieving goals are attributes which are encouraged and rewarded both at home and at school. Obviously this is not the kind of behavior which sees children being sent to school counselors, nor that which gets them punished by their parents.

These responsible children have learned to rely completely on themselves. It is what makes the most sense to them. They have learned the best way to achieve stability is to provide it for themselves. "If you want to get something done, do it yourself." They cannot consistently rely on mom or dad. The alcoholic and co-alcoholic may respond to the children emotionally and psychologically at times, but the unpredictability and inconsistency of the parents' behavior are the destructive elements.

Children also come to believe other adults will not be available to them when help is needed. Typically, they believe most adults are not capable, nor astute enough, to provide any insight or direction for their personal lives. Youngsters interpret this to mean others don't care, or aren't very sensitive. Such messages are internalized by the children; yet, possibly, never consciously acknowledged.

Most grown-ups perceive responsible children as very mature, dependable and very serious. These children are often viewed by peers as not quite so much fun as their other friends. These youngsters most typically either become active in structured social activities, or do not have significant social lives. They need to be in organized situations where they can be in control. Being goal-focused allows them a diversion from the family pain. This provides them psychological relief, and, they get positive feedback. Most importantly, at this time it does make their lives easier.

THE ADJUSTER

Put me in any situation now and I can adjust. But please don't ask me to be responsible for it or change it.

When others in the home provide structure, (typically an older sibling, mom or dad), younger children may not find it necessary to be responsible for themselves. The child called the adjuster finds it much easier to exist in this increasingly chaotic family situation by simply adjusting to whatever happens. This youngster does not attempt to prevent or alleviate any situation. The child doesn't think about the situation, or experience any emotions as a result of it. Whatever happens, when it happens, is simply handled. The adjuster's bottom line thinking is, "I can't do anything about it anyway," which in the child's mind seems to be a fairly realistic attitude. A professional person would describe the adjuster as the child who seems most detached from the family. The other children in the home perceive this child as more selfish while to the parents, this is the child they don't seem to notice as much.

While the responsible child and the placating child are very visible within the home, due to their interacting with other family members, the adjusting child is seen less often. This is the youngster who most likely goes to his room unannounced; who spends less time at home, and more time with his friends; this is the family member who seems oblivious of the conflicts and emotions at home.

As the child heads out the door to stay at a friend's house for the night, and dad hollers, "Where do you think you're going? Who gave you permission to go anywhere? You aren't going anywhere. You are staying right here tonight!", the adjuster simply comes back into the house, returns his clothes to the closet, and quietly calls his friend to give some excuse for not coming over. He knows dad had told him earlier in the day it was okay to spend the night at his friend's house, he also knows it won't do any good to argue with dad now that he has been drinking. This same child, when dad hasn't shown up for one single ballgame all season, simply tells mom it was no big deal, and not to feel bad, because he doesn't feel bad, "Besides, if dad had shown up, he probably would have been drunk anyway." It's just easier to accept the situation.

Children describe the many times mom gets tired and angry with dad because of his drinking, so she packs the children and their belongings in the car and races off to a relative's. The next day she packs them up again and they return home, because somehow mom and dad got things worked out. So, there they are, back home the very next day. Their clothes are back in the drawers, and they're all sitting at the dinner table--everyone acting if the previous night didn't happen. So many have told me, "It is just easier that way. It doesn't help to question it. And, it certainly doesn't help to interfere." Adjusting children find it wiser to follow, and simply not draw attention to themselves. This behavior is less painful for these children, and makes life easier for the rest of the family as well. The role of the adjuster is permeated with denial, without the focus on others. It is this lack of attention to others which makes adjusters appear to be more selfish.

Acting without thinking or feeling is typical of the true adjuster. Once, a young woman told me about the time she and her father had gone to a ballgame together, 30 miles from home. She said her father dropped her off at the game, and he went to a tavern. He was intoxicated when he picked her up after the game. She said this didn't cause her any concern, in fact, it was typical. But, this night, as they headed for home, he stopped at the only tavern, 15 miles away. He gave her the keys to the car and said, "Now, I want you to drive home and tell your mom I am at the D.B. Tavern, and I'll be home in a little while." The young girl got in the car and drove home. Even though she didn't know how to drive she didn't question her father or his instructions. She said, "He had left the car running, and it was an automatic. I just got in and pointed it toward home. I ran in and out of ditches and drove mostly on the shoulder, but I got home. I was crying the whole way home but when I got there I calmed myself down, went into the house, put the keys on the drainboard, walked into my mother's bedroom, told mom that dad was at the D.B. Tavern and would be home in awhile. I then went to my room and went to bed." She said both her father and mother knew she didn't drive; her father ignored the fact; her mother didn't even ask how she got home. She said "Once I got in the house, I didn't think about what had happened."

"Put me in any situation and I will handle it. I won't feel, get upset, or question it; I will just respond to it." The adjuster does not think of saying, "Dad, I can't drive home, I don't know how to drive." She doesn't want to get dad upset. She doesn't think of simply waiting for dad to come back. After all, she was given instructions and she has learned the best way to keep peace in the family is to respond to those instructions without question. She doesn't think of calling her mother and asking for advice on how to handle the situation--she does not want to cause her mother any problems. It is just so much safer to handle the situation alone.

At school, the adjusting child is as nondescript as he or she is at home. Academically, this child is about average, not demonstrating brilliance or ignorance, consequently not drawing any negative or positive attention through school work. Therefore, this child does not greatly impact or impress teachers in any way.

In social situations at school, the adjuster associates with other children, but does not take any leadership roles. Rather, the adjuster remains somewhat detached and in the outer parameters of social circles.

THE PLACATER

Whenever a family problem comes up, both sides will call me to settle disputes. I am called on to make many decisions, and I do them all alone. Many friends used to call me for advice as they felt that I "know" a lot and rarely had problems of my own.

In every home, there is usually at least one child who is particularly more sensitive--one who laughs harder, cries harder and seems to be more emotionally involved in everyday events. When parents talk about their children, it is typical to hear them identify one in particular as the "one who is more sensitive than the others." This is usually stated matter of factly, and accepted as being quite normal. In the alcoholic family, the placating child is not necessarily the only sensitive child in the home, but is the one perceived as the "most sensitive." This child's feelings are hurt more easily than the other childrens'! Yet, he likes to make others feel better. The placater finds the best way to cope, in this inconsistent and tension-filled home, is by acting in a way which will lessen his own tension and pain, as well as that of the other family members. This child will spend his early and adolescent years trying to "fix" the sadness, fears, angers and problems of brothers, sisters, and certainly, of mom and dad.

While mom and dad are arguing, and the other children are afraid of what will happen, the placater does something to diminish the fear. When a sibling is embarrassed by mom's drunken behavior at the supermarket, this most sensitive child acts to make the situation less painful for the sister. A brother is angry because dad broke another promise, this youngster reacts to help dispel the brother's anger. This pattern develops at a surprisingly young age, as demonstrated when 5-year-old Michael told his crying mom, "Don't worry mom, I won't remember all of this when I grow up." The placater is always there to make life easier for the others in the alcoholic home.

As this sensitive child grows to adulthood, others experience him as a "nice" person. After all, he spends his time trying to please others, trying to make others feel better, and usually he succeeds in doing just that. The placater becomes very skilled at listening and demonstrating empathy, and is well-liked for these attributes. If this child is a full-fledged placater, he will never disagree. In fact, he is the first to apoligize if he feels an apology is needed, especially if it will protect another person. Eleven-year-old Tom apologized to his mother on the average of 10-15 times a day -- "I'm sorry you broke the milk bottle." "I'm sorry you don't feel well," "I'm sorry I am 30 seconds late to the breakfast table." 'I am just plain sorry," Tom's mom was alcoholic, and Tommy said to me, "I just couldn't figure out why she was always drunk, and knew there must be something I did to make her so unhappy. So, I just tried to make it better by apologizing."

Parents are often proud of the placater, believing he knows how to share; they know he is not a selfish child. Too, they never have to worry about the placater being disappointed, because he doesn't appear to get upset when plans fall through and he doesn't let anyone know he is bothered by anything. Dad doesn't take the children to the game as he promised; the placating youngster squelches his own disappointment and focuses on his younger brother for the rest of the day. When mom says, "No" unjustifiably, the sensitive child may have tears well up in his eyes, but he takes them to his room to cry alone. He isn't going to argue or run to the other parent. In every way he seems to be a very warm, caring, nonproblem-causing, sensitive child.

Again, these sensitive characteristics are displayed at school just as they are at home. In fact these are the qualities which make the placating children so well-liked at school. Acting the role of the placater is certainly safe for them. If they allowed themselves to risk self disclosure, they would have to deal with their own reality, and experience the pain of that reality. So, these children are adept at diverting attention from themselves and focusing it onto other persons. Imagine the resultant personality when this role is combined with that of the responsible child -- the combination of the child responsible for the tangible environment and for the emotional needs of others. It is easy to understand why placaters are well-liked at school and at home; it is even easier to recognize why they don't draw attention to themselves.

ACTING OUT CHILD

As we have already discussed, most children raised in alcoholic homes react to the turmoil in their lives in a way which doesn't draw negative attention to them or to their family members. But, I also must make reference to those children who don't fit one, or a combination, of the three roles I've outlined so far. They may be children in the family who have been drawing attention to themselves by negative behavior. Instead of behaving in a manner which actually brings greater stability into their lives, or at least one which does not add to the turmoil, "acting out children" often display delinquent problematic behavior which more adequately typifies the state of the family. The acting-out child is the assumed stereotype in an alcoholic family. Acting-out children will cause disruption in their own lives and in the lives of other family members. In doing so, they will often provide distraction from the issue of alcoholism.

If there is a delinquent child in the family, it is often easier for parents to focus on that child and the ensuing problems created, rather than worry about dad's or mom's alcoholic drinking. Such children are the ones who are doing poorly or dropping out of school, getting pregnant in mid-teens, drinking at the age of 12, abusing other drugs and exhibiting other socially unacceptable behavior. They may be found in correctional facilities, mental hospitals, or other institutions during some time in their lives.

I want to acknowledge that certainly, with the estimated 12-15 million children being raised in alcoholic homes in the United States today, there are a large number who do fit the acting -out stereotype. The acting-out children are the ones most likely to be addressed and receive help from one or more professionals. And, most professionals who work with children in trouble -- teachers, social workers, police people, psychologists, judges, probation officers, chaplains -- tend to believe that these youngsters are products of their environment. Unacceptable behavior is learned, and parents are the primary role models in this learning process.

Parents usually set the mold, either through action or inaction. Most children in trouble have an extremely poor self-image reflecting the feeling they sense their parents have — inadequacy. Acting-out children find it nearly impossible to communicate their feelings to adults in a healthy way. While other children who have the same problems learn how to depress or repress problem areas and focus on other areas of their lives, acting-out children use unacceptable forms of behavior to say, "care about me," or "I can't cope."

Parental immaturity, often expressed in extreme selfishness, lack of consistency, cruel teasing or inappropriate discipline, are variables most often described in families of delinquents, and, more often after than not, are characteristic of life in alcoholic homes.

Where other children tend to either draw positive attention to themselves or escape attention, the acting-out child exacerbates his own situation by eliciting the kind of attention which causes parents to cry, nag, bluster, call the child names and, generally, undermine the child's self-esteem.

The opinions and acceptance of one's peers are extremely important to most teenagers, yet, most children of alcoholics are focused enough on home, or are detached enough to be less concerned with this peer acceptance. The sensitive acting-out child, however, who lacks the ability to detach or focus on other things, and lacks a strong parent-child relationship will gravitate toward peers -- peers who usually have equally low self-esteem.

Unfortunately, thousands of these acting-out children don't get help and, for those who do, the help they get is only for their problematic behavior, not for being part of an alcoholic family system which is the basis of their behavior.

* * * * * *

The bottom line is: ALL CHILDREN RAISED IN ALCOHOLIC HOMES NEED TO BE ADDRESSED. ALL CHILDREN ARE AF-FECTED. The next few chapters will describe how these children, who appear to be doing well in spite of the alcoholism in their homes, become alcoholic themselves, marry someone who is or becomes alcoholic, and/or as a peer of mine said, "just have enormous problems in adulthood."

CHAPTER 3

Don't Talk
Don't Trust
Don't Feel

The Best Little Boy in the World (He Won't Tell)

By Peter M. Nardi

Michael was doing very well in school. In fact, he was the brightest kid in class, the teacher's favorite, one of the best-behaved. He never created any disciplinary problems and always hung out with the good crowd. The best little boy in the world. "Why can't we all be like Michael and sit quietly?" Sister Gertrude would say in her most melodious voice. Conform, be docile, do well, be quiet. Hold it in. Don't tell a soul.

And now he was waiting at the school corner for his mother to pick him up. This was always the hardest moment. What will she look like, how will she sound? Michael could tell right away if she had been drinking. The muffled voice, the pale, unmade-up face. He really didn't know what it was all about. He just knew that when Dad came home he would fight with her. Argue, yell, scream, run. Michael could hear them through the closed doors and over the humming of the air conditioner. He wondered if the neighbors could hear, too. Hold it in. Don't tell anyone.

He was still waiting at the corner. She was 15 minutes late. It was so good to go to school and get out of the house. But when 3 o'clock came he would feel the tension begin to gather inside him. He never knew what to expect. When she was not drinking, she would be smiling, even pretty. When drunk, she'd be cold, withdrawn, tired, unloving, not caring. Michael would cook dinner and straighten up the house. He would search for the alcohol, like egg-hunting on Easter morning, under the stuffed chair in the bedroom in the laundry bag concealed among the towels, behind her hats in the closet. When he found it, he'd pour it down the sink drain. Maybe then no one would know that she'd been drinking. Maybe no one would fight. Don't tell a soul.

She still hadn't come to pick him up yet. She'd never been 30 minutes late. Sometimes she'd sleep late in the morning after Dad had already left for work, and Michael would make breakfast for his little sister and himself. Then a friend's mother would take them to school. The biggest problem was during vacation time, especially around the holidays. He wanted to play with his friends. But he was afraid to bring them home. He was afraid to go out and play, too, because then she would drink. Michael didn't want to be blamed for that. So he stayed in and did his homework and read. He didn't tell his friends. Hold it in.

And still he was waiting alone on the corner. Forty-five minutes late. Michael decided to walk the 10 blocks home. He felt that he was old enough now. After all, he took care of his little sister a lot. He took care of his mother a lot. He was responsible. He always did what people told him to do. Everyone could count on him for help. Everyone did. And he never complained. Never fought, never argued, never yelled. The best little boy in the world. Hold it in.

When he got nearer to home, Michael's heart felt as if it were going to explode. Her car was there, the house was locked tight. He rang the bell. He rang and rang as he felt his stomach turn inside out. He climbed through a window. No one seemed to be home. He looked around the house, in all the right hiding places. Finally, in the closet in his own bedroom, he saw his mom in her slip, with a belt around her neck, and attached to the wooden rod. She was just sitting there, sobbing. She had been drinking. But maybe no one would find out. Michael wouldn't tell anyone, ever. Hold it in.

Thousands of children are being, or have been, raised in homes where at least one parent is alcoholic, and appear as children to suffer no apparent ill effects. These young people usually do not leave home prematurely. They are typical in that, as most children, they leave home at the ages of 17, 18 or 19. In venturing out on their own, they face the task of making decisions common to young people at these ages. They make choices about careers, lifestyles, friends, where, and with whom they are going to live, and, possibly, whether or not to enter a branch of the military. They often make decisions about marriage, and many make decisions about having children.

These children of alcoholics, along with thousands of other young people, begin to not only make some of the most important decisions of their lives, but to spend a number of years implementing those decisions. Typically, it will take the next six to eight years to implement and follow through with these career and family decisions. During this time, young adults focus on external events. It is not normally a time when they sit back and contemplate how good or poor the past years were for them. As young adult children of alcoholics leave home, (many having recognized the alcoholism, others not yet identifying it for what it is) they breathe a sigh of relief and pat themselves on the back for having survived. They then begin going about their own lives, but usually continue to stay socially and emotionally entangled with their family.

It is about this time, when a young person reaches the mid-twenties that the effects of growing up in an alcoholic home begin to become apparent. These now adult children of alcoholics begin to experience a loneliness which doesn't make sense to them. They become aware of feelings which separate them from others, and find themselves depressed. As this depression occurs more frequently and lasts longer, the source of depression seems unidentifiable. Feelings of being fearful and anxious occur more frequently; again, the source is not identifiable. They have problems related to intimacy; they find themselves having difficulty maintaining a close relationship, or find that something seems to be missing in their relationships. A lack of meaningfulness begins to permeate every aspect of their lives. And, very possibly, they are beginning to drink more, or they already find themselves in a relationship with someone who could become or is, an alcoholic.

It is very important to look back at the processes which have occurred and, typically, have not been recognized, let alone addressed, for this very special person -- the child raised in an alcoholic home.

DON'T TALK

The Family Law: DON'T TALK ABOUT THE REAL ISSUES. The real issues are: Mom is drinking again. Dad didn't come home last night. Dad was drunk at the ballgame. I had to walk home from school because Mom had passed out at home and forgot to come and get me.

Some say it is a rule; I believe, for most alcoholic families, it has become law. As one 9-year-old daughter of an alcoholic said, "When you have a rule in your house for so long, to not talk about dad's drinking, it's r-e-a-l-l-y hard to talk now (even when he is sober)."

In the earlier stages of alcoholism, when someone's drinking seems to become a more noticeable problem, family members usually attempt to rationalize the behavior. They begin to invent excuses: "Well, your dad has been working hard these past few months," or, "your mom has been lonely since her best friend moved away." As the drinking increases, the drinking and the irrational rationalizations become a "normal" way of life. Family members focus on the problems drinking causes but, have difficulty associating drinking with those problems. An excuse offered to a child I had been working with for her dad's irrational (alcoholic) behavior, was that he had a brain tumor and was going to die. The mother told the children their father wanted them to hate him before he died, so it would be easier for them to accept his death when it happened. This now adult person explains, "It didn't feel right, but who was I to question my mom? She had enough problems as it was." As a child, this woman believed her father was going crazy. She felt "his going crazy seemed more likely than his going to die from a tumor." She now understands her father acted crazy, but his erratic behavior was due to his drinking. His increasingly controlling and tyrannical moods, his inconsistent behavior related to his blackouts, as well as his open hallucinations, added to his appearance of craziness.

It is easier to invent reasons, other than alcoholism, for crazy behavior. If the drinking takes place outside of the home, and dad doesn't act falling-down drunk when he comes home, or if they don't see him when he comes home, the children may more readily accept what the other parent tells them -- drinking is not the problem.

If children do not understand alcoholism, it is difficult for them to identify their parent as alcoholic. Children are like adults in that, they too, will believe all alcoholics are old men on Skid Row, without jobs or families. One adult person said, "My dad loved me, and I knew that." No one ever explained to her that alcoholic people are also capable of loving others. She believed because her father loved her he could not be alcoholic. She heard about alcoholism only once at church where a recovering alcoholic told his story. But, what she heard was that particular alcoholic's perception of his own drinking. She could not relate this same type of alcoholism to her father's drinking. Her father certainly didn't sound, look, or act like this man who had been her only other contact with an alcoholic. Such fragmented information is typical of childrens' lack of knowledge concerning the disease of alcoholism.

Another way which helps family members rationalize the alcoholic's behavior is for them to not discuss or, in any manner, talk about what's really happening at home. Thirteen-year-old Steve said, "I thought I was going crazy. I thought I was the only one in my house who knew dad was an alcoholic. I didn't know anyone else knew." I asked him why he believed this to be true. He answered, "because no one else ever said anything." Steve described an incident which occurred when he and his father were at home alone. His father, in a semi-conscious state from drunkeness, was on the floor, had thrown-up, hit his head on the coffee table and was bleeding. Steve's mother and sisters had returned home within moments after his dad had hit his head. They just picked dad up and carried him off to the bedroom. No one spoke to anyone else. Steve said again he thought, "maybe this is all in my head." I asked the two older sisters and Steve's mother why they had not talked about this incident with Steve. They responded, "because he hadn't said anything, and we hoped he hadn't noticed." I believe helplessness, despair and hopelessness cause family members to believe -- if you just ignore it, maybe it will not hurt; if you just ignore it, it may just go away.

Many adult children have told me they were instructed not to talk about things which would upset mom or dad; or they simply learned by themselves that things went much easier when they did nothing to "rock the boat." One young man said, "dinner was pretty quiet. Anything we said rocked the boat. And then, if we were too quiet, that rocked the boat!" These children not only don't talk about boat rocking issues, but they don't talk about, or share, their fears, worries or hurts with anyone.

Children will share the same bedroom with a sibling for years, both hearing the arguing taking place between mom and dad. Or, they hear mom crying night after night. But they only hear, they never speak to one another about it, although they may each cry --silently and alone. In one family, the six children were between the ages of 12 and 21 when dad sought treatment for his alcoholism. Three to four months prior to seeking help, the father would return home late at night after having been drinking for several hours. Not having seen his children all day, he'd make his nightly rounds, passing from one room to another, until he'd seen each of his children. He would scream, shout and harass each child before moving on to the next room. All of the children were awake as he went from room to room but they never spoke to each other about these nightly episodes. The family simply acted as though nothing out of the ordinary was happening.

In another family, young Billy told me how he was taking the air out of the car tires so dad wouldn't drive when he was drinking. His youngest sister, Ann, was putting water in dad's vodka bottle; his oldest sister, Lisa, was putting apple cider in dad's whiskey. Each was unaware of the other's actions concerning dad's drinking because they were unable to talk about the real issue -- their father's alcoholism.

Well-adjusted children who experience daily childhood problems would, most likely, talk about these problems with other family members. Because of the denial of the alcoholism in an alcoholic family, seldom are any of the children's problems recognized, and the family problem -- alcoholism -- is never discussed. These children (accurately or inaccurately) do not perceive others, inside or outside of the family, to be available to them for help. Many adult children of alcoholics have questioned where their aunts and uncles were when they needed them. Many wondered why grandpa and grandma weren't more concerned for them. Nora, another adult child told me if she had told anybody what her home life was like, she couldn't possibly have been believed. "They wouldn't believe me, because if it was so bad, I couldn't be looking so good. They never saw my mother getting drunk every day, they never saw her raving like a maniac, passed out upstairs. They never saw her bottles all over the house. They just never saw."

While many children fear not being believed, they may also experience guilt talking about the problems of their parents. They feel a sense of betrayal in talking about such delicate problems. Children find the family situation so complex and confusing, they feel inadequate in attempting to verbalize the problems --they just don't know how to tell others. Children feel very loyal to their parent, and invariably, they end up defending their parents, rationalizing that it isn't really all that bad, and continuing in what has now become a denial process.

It is most despairing to be a child in an alcoholic family, to feel totally alone, and to believe talking to someone will not help.

Sometimes I pretend my mom is not drinking when she really is. I never even talk about it.
                                         Melody -- Age 9

I Won't Tell

These two tiny spoons used to be set
in small bowls of salt on my grandmother's
dining room table. They come from Tilden-
Thurber Silversmiths in Providence, Rhode
Island. Her name was Eugenia Price Brewster

and would she ever be surprised at her son
Benjamin's house. It all came back this
afternoon when a stray jar of blackberry
jam was discovered behind my bran flakes.

I made it with berries picked two Octobers
ago. In his backyard bushes were full
of the dark ripe fruit. I set them one
by one into the bucket and wondered why
he let so many vodka bottles cover his floor

so many of his mother's bone china dishes
serve as ashtrays. Ashtrays?
Burial grounds for so many cigarettes
some people wouldn't believe me. The empty
half-gallon of Thunderbird wine was filled

to within one inch of its top and it
was sitting in the blue and white flowered
Copenhagen bowl that used to be piled
high with fluffy potatoes whose Thanksgiving
gravy was sprinkled with the diminutive
salt spoons. She'd be amazed.

Joan, adult child

DON'T TRUST

*I am always on my guard with people. I want to
trust them, but it is so much easier to just rely on
myself. I'm never sure what other people want.*

Children raised in alcoholic family structures have learned
how to not trust others in talking about the real issues. They have
also learned it is simply best to not trust that others will be there
for them, emotionally, psychologically, and possibly even
physically. To trust another means investing confidence,
reliance, and faith in that person. Confidence, reliance and
faithfulness are virtues often missing in the alcoholic home.
Children need to be able to depend on parents to meet their
physical and emotional needs in order to develop trust. In
alcoholic environments, parents simply are not consistently
available to their children either by being drunk, physically absent, or mentally and emotionally preoccupied with alcohol, or
with the alcoholic. Again, it needs to be noted that in talking
about children in alcoholic homes I am talking about children
responding to <u>both</u> the drinking and the enabling
parent. These children respond to the alcoholic family system on
the whole.

- Joan can't count on her mom to be attentive about what she
has to say after coming home from school. Joan's mom doesn't
smile after hearing about something funny which happened to
Joan at school, nor is her mom very sensitive to her sadnesses.
Usually, Joan's mom is preoccupied with what happened last
night, or what didn't happen last night, as the result of dad's
drinking.

- Carl doesn't trust people to see his feelings as important. He
may be angry about something that happened on the way home
from school, but he usually doesn't say anything about it
because, "There's enough to be angry about at home. Who needs
more? Besides, they wouldn't understand."

- Bill cannot trust decisions his parents make. He told me he can't rely on his dad to remember a promise to go for a drive on the weekend, or giving Bill approval to spend an evening at a friend's house. Nor can Bill count on his mom to support him if dad goes back on his word.

- Karen cannot rely on her mom to be sober for her birthday, Thanksgiving or Christmas.

- While Karen cannot rely on her mom for sobriety during special occasions, Jack knows his mother will drink on those holidays. He said the uncertainty, the never knowing for sure how dad was going to handle mom's drunkenness, was most confusing for him.

Allen, age 32, told me of a time when he was 11 years old. He had returned home from school and found his mother intoxicated. As he came through the door, she started an argument with him. She began to scream and shout at him, and he began to scream and shout back. This was a typical after-school scene but, this time, mom picked up a broom and began hitting him about the head and shoulders. While mom was screaming and hitting, Allen was ducking and hollering back at her. He ran to the telephone and called his father. (Allen's father lived away from home.) Allen was surprised when his father answered, but he did at least answer! Imagine the scene of an 11-year-old Allen yelling into the phone explaining what was happening, ducking the broom, while his mom screamed at him and continued hitting him. . .his father shouted back into the receiver, "Don't worry, she won't remember it tomorrow."

Twenty-one years later, when Allen related this incident to me, he spoke with no affect or expression in his voice. I responded saying, "Allen, does that sound like a normal response to you?" Allen looked at me quizically and said slowly, "Normal? I don't know. I guess I have never really thought about it." Of course Allen had not thought about it. Allen could not rely on his mother to be there, to respond emotionally, psychologically or physically, or to meet his needs in any way when he was a 11-year-old boy. Allen could not rely on his father to understand his needs, let alone offer protection, while he was being physically abused. Allen wouldn't find it emotionally safe to allow himself to respond with hurt, anger, or disgust to either his mother's beating or his father's lack of concern. But, Allen did find it safe to detach himself, and to not think about the incident. Allen, like so many others, learned through similar experiences, not to trust.

In order for children to trust, they must feel safe. They need to be able to depend on their parents for friendly help, concern and guidance in responding to physical and emotional needs. Yet, in alcoholic homes, children often cannot rely on parents to provide any of this "safety."

A child tells of how he never feels safe "bringing friends home" because, "it's always possible mom will be drunk and do something to embarrass me." Another says it is never safe even to play in our own yard, because "Dad always seems to be sure to belittle me when my friends are around." These children live in a fearful environment. For some, their "safety" is more psychological; for others, it is psychological and physical. Children often tell of frightening times with the drinking alcoholic when he is driving recklessly, or when fires are caused due to drunken neglect. Children's physical safety is often direct-ly threatened when verbal harassment turns violent, when fur-niture is being broken, or certainly when persons in the home are actually physically and/or sexually assaulted.

It is difficult to trust a person who repeatedly embarrasses, humiliates, disappoints, or puts you in physical jeopardy. It is even more difficult to trust, or attempt to regain trust, when peo-ple aren't talking about incidents which are occurring in the home -- when family members minimize, rationalize, and/or blatantly deny certain events are taking place.

Part of feeling safe is feeling secure. The feeling of security is seldom present for any length of time in alcoholic homes. Tim comes home from school one day to discover dad has lost his job again for the fourth time in three years. It means the family will be moving again. For Tim, it means giving up some new-found friends at a school which was just beginning to become familiar to him. And it means giving up the opportunity to make more friends through the little league he just joined. . .another disappointment. Tammy finds out her dad gave away her pure-bred pet rabbits to a drinking buddy. She had been raising them from bunnies with the intention of entering them in the county fair that fall. . .another hope shattered. David learns the family's long planned summer vacation has to be cancelled because dad loaned the vacation money to a stranger he met at a local bar. . . another promise broken. Children continually are confronted with reasons to be insecure in their surroundings, to not trust.

One adult child described his inability to trust this way: "Trust? My dad couldn't ever seem to take care of himself wherever he was. There was always a problem -- at home, at work, with the car, with grandparents, with friends. If he couldn't take care of himself, how was he going to take care of me? No, I couldn't trust him for anything. And my mom, she was there, but that's all I can say. She was physically there, but I don't remember her ever trying to help us cope or understand. She was simply there."

Children being raised in alcoholic homes constantly hear mixed messages. . .messages which teach distrust. A parent often gives a child false information intentionally, in a feeble effort to protect the child from reality. A mother may tell the children she is happy when she is actually miserable. A father may reassure a child that nothing is wrong when the child can see mother is acting strangely. The child is confused because one message is coming from his parent's words, and a contradictory message from the body movement and tone of voice. Such confusing messages propel the child into a life of second guessing what is really happening.

The single-most important ingredient in a nurturing relationship -- in any relationship -- is honesty. No child can trust, or be expected to trust, unless those around him are also open and honest about their own feelings. Alcoholics lose this ability to be honest as their disease progresses. As the alcoholic continues to drink, he has to rationalize his negative behavior and he has to do it extremely well in order to continue his drinking. An alcoholic's life is consumed with feelings of guilt, shame, anxiety, and remorse causing him to drink all that much more to attempt an escape. It becomes a never-ending circle because of the psychological need to drink, and a physical addiction to alcohol. Enabling parents are fearful of being honest with their children. They don't want them to experience the same pain they are feeling; and they don't want to acknowledge that the problem exists in the first place.

While children don't require verbalization of all the feelings their parents experience, they do need validation and/or clarification of certain specific situations and feelings. This validation or clarification doesn't happen in a home where NOT TALKING AND NOT TRUSTING permeate.

A person takes a risk when he reaches out to trust another. Those persons who have learned to take the risk have experienced trusting to be a good process. They have also experienced a sense of security and a feeling of self-worth which are both derived from feeling loved. All young people need to feel valued, to feel they are precious and special. While parents may speak to children and tell them they are special and loved, it is the parents' behavior which must substantiate the spoken word -- it is behavior which allows a child to believe.

Children need focused attention. Focused attention represents not only physically being with a child, but interacting with the child in a way which says, "You have all of my attention -- mentally and emotionally." Focused attention says to a child, "I care. It's important for me to be with you." Children are highly sensitive to the degree of focused attention they receive. A child receives no sense of value from parents who are forever absorbed in their own affairs. While children don't need exclusive attention, it is a lack of focused attention -- when others never have time to truly be with them -- which causes them to feel unimportant. As a parent's disease of alcoholism progresses and the need for, and the preoccupation with, alcohol becomes greater, the denial and the isolation from others due to the emotional turmoil within makes the alcoholic less frequently available to his or her children. As well, the co-alcoholic becomes increasingly preoccupied with the alcoholic and her own helplessness and hopelessness, thus decreasing their availability as a resource for the child.

Although these children are not totally ignored, as the alcoholism and co-alcoholism progresses the availability of focused time decreases. When these families do spend time together, that time is often centered around drinking. Tim, age 15, told of how he was spending "special time" with his father. Both liked to fish and did so quite often during the summer. But, although Tim always looked forward to the two of them spending time alone together, he was almost always disappointed because dad normally brought along a drinking buddy. Dad and his buddy got so involved in their drinking and carrying on Tim might as well have been totally alone. Tim spent time with his dad, but the time spent did not allow Tim that "special time" meant just for him and his father. The father's attention was always focused elsewhere -- with or without Tim around.

Children need focused attention most when they are under stress. Unfortunately, often in an alcoholic environment this is when they are least apt to receive focused attention. Stress often becomes the norm in this environment and it is very typical that the attention will then center around the alcoholic in the home. Thus, instead of turning attention to the child who may be having a problem, attention is turned away from the child, and the child's problem is never addressed.

Children often find they do not trust caring acts and focused attention when they do occur. Because of broken promises and not being able to rely on consistency of positive interaction children are often confused by them and many times, don't trust the motivation behind them.

A child may enjoy a trip to the zoo, but will question the motivation behind the trip. Although both parents may have agreed on the excursion out of sincere caring, the child perceives only the alcoholic parent's sense of guilt, or the co-alcoholic's dominance in the situation. The child thinks maybe the parents do care in this one instance, but that feeling is overshadowed by the knowledge that neither parent may be relied on to be available at another important time in his or her life. And, they may always wonder, "Did dad bring me this present because he didn't come to my piano recital last night, or because he saw it and wanted me to have it out of his love for me?"

While children in alcoholic homes can and do survive, problems arise in their lives because their environmental circumstances have made it impossible for them to feel safe and secure, or to rely on or trust others. Trust is one of those vital character-building blocks children need in order to develop into healthy adults. Being raised in an alcoholic family structure often denies or distorts this portion of a child's development.

> *I have a hard time trusting my mom.*
>
> *Chuck -- Age 6*

DON'T FEEL

> *No I wasn't embarassed. I was scared for my father, but I wasn't scared for myself. It didn't dawn on me to be scared for me. I wasn't disappointed. I didn't really think about it. I never got angry at him. There was nothing to get angry about. I didn't cry much. What was there to cry about?*

It has been my experience that by the time a child being raised in an alcoholic family reaches the age of 9, he has a well-developed denial system about both his feelings and his perceptions of what is happening in the home. The above statements say, "No, I don't feel. And if I do, it is a feeling for someone else. I can feel scared for my father or my sister, but not for myself." As one 9-year-old said to me, "One time, my dad got upset when he was drinking, and he slapped me. I looked at my mom and she started crying. So I cried. I wasn't crying for me, I was crying for mom."

Children raised in alcoholic homes do whatever they possibly can to bring stability and consistency into their lives. They will behave in a manner which makes it easier for them to cope, easier for them to survive. The role adoption described in the first chapter assists these children in coping with the inconsistencies in their lives. Learning to focus on the environment or on other people, or learning to detach oneself from the family, assists children in not feeling.

The alcoholic family's law of DON'T TALK and the premise DON'T TRUST teach children it isn't safe to share feelings either. Children learn not to share their feelings and, inevitably, learn to deny feelings because they don't trust these feelings will be validated by family members, other relatives, or friends. They don't trust their feelings will get the necessary nurturing. Children of alcoholics don't perceive others as resources, therefore, they live their lives alone. Being isolated with feelings of fear, worry, embarassment, guilt, anger, lonelines, etc., leads to a state of desperation, of being overwhelmed. Such a state of being does not lend itself to survival, so the children learn other ways to cope. They learn how to discount and repress feelings, and some learn simply not to feel. These children do have access to their feelings, but only with the help of a trusted person. However, for the majority of children of alcoholics, trust and trusted persons are not a consistent part of their lives.

Kathy is a cheerleader for her high school's basketball team. One evening, at an out-of-town game, her father arrived noticeably drunk. Were Kathy raised in a healthy family, she would naturally be embarrassed and humiliated witnessing her father's drunken behavior. She would be even more embarrassed if he draped himself over her and spoke loudly to the crowd of jeering kids in the stands. Then, as Kathy attempted to more-or-less carry him from the gymnasium, she would only naturally fear that the kids would begin directing their jeering attention on her. In addition, Kathy would probably be angry with her mother for allowing this situation to develop. Embarrassment, humiliation, fear, and anger are the normal emotions a child in this situation would experience.

But for Kathy, who is being raised in an alcoholic home, none of these emotions are conducive to her perception of how to

handle the problem. Instead, the reaction of this most responsible eldest child was to take care of the situation, and to get her
father out of the gymnasium before he got hurt.

Kathy has learned if she lets feelings take over when an incident like the one just mentioned occurs, it will only result in pain
for herself. It doesn't occur to her to talk to anyone (a chaperone
on the trip, a school friend) about the incident because she
believes no one would really understand, worse yet, that they
would only make unkind judgments about her and her father.

For Kathy, only a few tears fell as she headed home on the pep
bus that night. None of her schoolmates mentioned the incident
and she most certainly didn't tell her mother about it. She knew that
to discuss the incident would only bring more pain to the family.
Kathy has found it's a lot "safer" to ignore her feelings. For her, the
feelings are too confusing, too complicated, and very scary. And,
she hasn't found anyone she can trust to share those scared feelings with.

Any young football player would feel disappointed if his dad
didn't show up for at least one game in the entire season. A child
from a healthy family would not only be disappointed, but angry as
well. But, for the child of an alcoholic father, this is just another one
of those events to try not to feel bad about. It is easier not to feel
anything than to dwell on the pain or the unfairness of it. And, if the
child does feel, it is easier to be angry with the nonalcoholic parent
when he or she misses one game, or to take the anger out on the
player who messed up a particular play.

Again, it would be normal for Jerry to be disappointed, afraid
and angry when, as a child, he has been sent to stay with a
relative because mom's drinking became worse. He has been
told, when he returns in a couple of weeks, mom won't be drinking. But, when he does return, Jerry finds his mother exactly the
way she was when he left home -- drunk. The 6-year-old Jerry in
this situation might tell dad he is angry (he hasn't yet learned to
deny). But, most likely, Jerry at age 9, would just ignore it; he
simply no longer allows himself to respond emotionally.

In these incidents of denial, the children are building walls of self-protection. They are learning coping mechanisms to protect themselves from fear -- fear of reality. The reality is that their parents are failing them. As the disease of alcoholism progresses, alcohol becomes the parents' obsession. When family members experience the results of this obsession, they ask the questions, "Why?" "Why does my mom disappoint me at important times?" "Why does my dad embarrass me like that?" "Doesn't he love me?" "Why is my dad drinking so much?" "Are my parents ever going to get better?" "Is she crazy?" "Is it my fault?" "Am I crazy?" It is frightening for family members to ask those questions of themselves. It can be even more frightening to allow themselves to answer them.

There is so much to feel about, to be emotional about, in an alcoholic family:

Afraid--   -to ask mom when dad will be coming home, to find out he may not
              -to tell Mom "no" for anything, for fear she'll get drunk.
              -of driving with mom when she is drinking
              -of getting hit when dad is drunk and violent
              -when mom and dad fight

Sad--   -because we didn't have any money, Dad could never keep a job
              -when I see my mother crying
              -when I have to sit in the car for hours and hours when dad is in the bar

Angry--   -at my dad, for making excuses for my mom when she is just drunk
              -at others, for calling my mom a drunk
              -at dad, for making promises and always breaking
              -them

Embarrassed--when I asked mom to attend a school function
              -and she showed up intoxicated
              -because dad has passed out in the front yard
              -because mom looks so sloppy, half-dressed

Guilty--   thinking if you hadn't talked back to your mother
                this morning, she might not have gotten drunk
                -for never being able to do enough to please my dad
                -for hating someone I was supposed to love, my mom
                -for being ashamed of my parents
                -for "being alive"

These are only a few of the multitude of feelings family members
may experience on a daily basis, yet learn not to express. As a
result, these persons often learn to discount, and inevitably deny
those feelings entirely. The reason for denying is to convince
themselves, as well as others, that their unhappy family life can be
made happy, by pretending, by denying reality. People tend to deny
and minimize both situations and feelings in order to hide their own
pain; they don't want to be uncomfortable. It is this ability to deny
which ultimately interferes in the emotional and psychological
stability of children of alcoholics when they reach adulthood.

> *John, why do you think other people feel angry,*
> *scared and disappointed, but you don't?*
> *Maybe because I have to be tough!*
> *John -- Age 13*

CHAPTER 4

The Progression of The Roles

CHAPTER FOUR

Children raised in alcoholic homes enter adulthood coping with life's problems in ways which have proven to be of great value to them; such as being responsible, adjusting, or placating, as well as not talking, not feeling and not trusting. A significant dynamic that has occurred is that they all have made some decisions about their own drinking. And as the majority of Americans do most have decided that they will drink. They decide at about the same ages and for the same reasons that children of non-alcoholic families choose to drink. These youngsters usually begin to drink in their early teens, drinking to have fun, drinking because friends want them to, drinking out of curiosity, and for some drinking out of defiance. They want to drink to feel grown-up. They learn to drink to escape. As typical of most teen-agers they often drink to get drunk. They are experimenting. But most significantly, they drink with an extra belief — a belief that "it will never happen to me." This is a belief that ascribes to their knowing that their parent is alcoholic but believing that alcoholism is a matter of lack of will power, that it is a control issue. This belief says, "I have seen enough and I know enough about what alcohol can do to a person. I will be different."

THE RESPONSIBLE ONE

As adults, they find no reason to change these patterns which have always ensured survival. Reaching young adulthood, children of alcoholics go on about their lives continuing to applaud themselves for being survivors. The oldest, or only child, the one who became the little adult, continues into the grown-up world carrying a lot of responsibility. The ability to be responsible has been a great strength, in that this young adult has already demonstrated a maturity in handling many different kinds of situations. He or she continues to take charge, and often assumes leadership roles. As a child, this person had learned to set realistic goals during his very early years, and as a young adult, he or she has realized a number of accomplishments far sooner than most people. But, there has been an evolution. This adult person experiences increasing anxiety, has become tense, and often feels separated from others by an invisible wall.

During their adolescent years, the children who adopted the responsible role were so busy being young adults, there was not time to be left to be children. Now, as adults, they don't find the joke all that funny. They didn't have time to relax as children and, as a consequence, they don't know how to relax as adults. As adolescents these responsible children of alcoholics had been taking life so seriously for so many years that now, in adulthood, they are awkward and uncomfortable with frivolity.

> *I still try to take alot of responsibility for people and things. I am only beginning to learn how to play. I find it difficult to enjoy hobbies of fun activities with any great consistency.*
>
> *Chris — age 32*

Chris, the responsible child, had so organized and structured her own childhood, she became a very rigid person, lacking in flexibility. As a child, Chris needed to be in charge, or at least feel she was in control; if she was not, she had a sense that her entire world was collapsing around her. For Chris, the adult, this phenomenon continues. She finds herself needing to take charge, to feel in absolute control, or there is a pervasive sense of losing control and being totally overwhelmed.

> *The idea of loss of control is intolerable to me. I get panicky when I try to think of it.*
>
> *Joe — age 33*

Joe tries to fit himself in structured positions and, ideally for him, positions he is able to control. Joe has to be in charge. He has to be in the one-up position, while someone else always has to be in the one-down position. There is not room in Joe's life for an equal relationship because that would mean giving up ultimate control which, for him, would be giving up on survival.

One-up, one-down, win-lose relationships are common in many

professional, social and intimate relationships. Remember, those responsible youngsters have become very rigid, serious, goal attaining young adults who have confidence in their ability to accomplish a great deal. These adults speak well (a skill learned as youngsters), and have mastered the ability to mask the reality of their earlier family life. No sense of equal relaitonships exists for these persons, nor does a sense of problem solving. For these responsible adult children everything is black or white, one way or the other, with no in-between.

An example is a 31-year-old woman I was working with who was the only child of an alcoholic father. At the age of 31, she had succeeded in qualifying in a male dominated profession, and had become a lawyer in private practice, an apparent success. Unfortunately, she was alone in that private practice, because two attempts at working with other professionals had failed. She had no close female friends, and her third attempt at marriage was failing. She had developed those traits similar to so many other children of alcoholics who had not learned to trust that other people would be there for them when they were needed. She, as others who found it necessary to take on this responsible role, found it easier to rely on herself. So, here you have an accomplished person, outwardly successful, yet inwardly, someone who cannot bring herself to trust that others will be there for her. She can't depend on others, and therefore has no recourse but to relate on an unequal basis. She doesn't know how to have fun, nor can she talk about the real issues for herself, and she certainly can't talk about her feelings. In her personal and professional relationships, this responsible person is almost forced to associate with others who are equally emotionally inaccessible. Should she find a very feeling, articulate, open, caring, fun loving person in her life, she would not know how to respond. The kind of sharing, intimate relationship such a person would create, would be too uncomfortable; the responsible one removes herself or himself from that type of relationship. In fact, responsible children of alcoholics will align themselves with people who allow them to continue to be rigid, serious and unfeeling. Either that, or they separate themselves from others completely and continue to pursue very isolated lifestyles.

It is easy to see why many responsible children of alcoholics, who are now young adults, find themselves depressed, lonely, anxious, tense and fearful. It is also easy to see how and why they often enter into unhealthy personal relationships. Further, should these persons drink at all (and most do), it becomes apparent alcohol does something for them beyond what it does for the normal social drinker. Alcohol helps these persons become less rigid, loosen up, and relax. When they drink, they aren't quite so serious. Although these same personality changes occur in most normal people who drink, for those who are stuck in unhealthy patterns, alcohol may be the only thing which can provide relief. Taking a drink makes them feel adequate. . .a feeling which to be sustained leads from one drink to another and then another. When these individuals drink, they are able to become more open with their feelings, they show some vulnerability, and they discover that other people respond to them more positively when they exhibit this relaxed and open manner. This does not necessarily make them alcoholic, but it does reinforce their need to drink, and it can create a psychological dependency.

> *I was the all American kid. In high school, I maintained a 3.6 grade point average, and was a star on the championship baseball team. I was always trying to please my parents (dad was alcoholic and a compulsive gambler. Mom worked seven-days-a-week to support the family). After high school, I went into business for myself, but something was wrong. I was empty inside, didn't know why. Whatever I did just wasn't good enough. The more I achieved, the worse I felt. The accomplishment didn't mean anything. I couldn't fill the emptiness, it was always there. Finally, I couldn't face life anymore and had to turn to drugs and alcohol.*
>
> *Dean F.*

THE ADJUSTER

Those children who found it so much easier to shrug their shoulders and withdraw upstairs to the bedroom, or slip out to a friend's house, usually continue these survival patterns into their grown-up years. Adult adjusters find it easier to avoid positions where they need to take control. They function better if they take whatever occurs in stride. They have become adept at adjusting, being flexible and spontaneous, and they find pride in these traits. As one man told me, "I went to nine different schools as a kid. I never knew how long I would stay, or where I was going next. It wasn't bad, I learned how to make friends quickly. I met a lot of interesting people." Now, as an adult, this person finds it necessary to keep moving. "I get bored in one spot. I get bored if I am at a job more than nine months. I get bored with the same woman after nine months. I am even getting bored with this city. I have been here two years now."

Mom and Dad play tug of war with me. I Love them both and want them to be Good to each other. I feel Guilty and sad Alot cause I don't Know what to do so things will Get better and All of us can be HAPPY.

My Brother won't play tug of war. I Don't want to but I can't Get away.

Victoria, age 16

What happened for these children who adopted the adjusting pattern is that they had neither the opportunity to develop trust on an on-going basis, nor were they able to develop healthy relationships. All their lives, they seemed to be jumping in at the middle. It was difficult for them to identify a beginning, and they never knew how long a particular phase, or situation, would last. These now adults, who as kids never knew how long they would be living in one place, or how long mom would be sober this time, or how long dad would be staying away, learned how to handle, (or adjust) to whatever situation they were currently in.

The adult adjusters often have neither a sense of direction, nor do they have a sense of taking responsibility for the direction they would like their lives to take. They feel no sense of choice, and no sense of power over their own lives.

While the more responsible children of alcoholics have developed a sense of being able to affect the events in their lives, adjusters usually do not have a sense of control. As 44-year-old Janice says, "I feel like I have been on a roller coaster for a real long time."

For adjusting children, life is a perpetual roller coaster -- not because they like living that way, but because they feel they have no other options. They perceive themselves as having no alternatives; they never learned that choices were available to them. So now, as adults, they don't talk about real issues in their lives, and they certainly do not seriously examine their own feelings. Adjusters find themselves associating with others who are as emotionally closed as they are. To them, this limited association is the only type of relationship which is safe.

Based on this behavior pattern, it is easy to see how adjusters find mates who cause uproar. This state of living in constant agitation becomes their comfort zone because they are perpetuating childhood roles of adapting to inconsistent people. They know how to handle chaotic situations -- adjust. Yet, this kind of self-negating adjusting results in the person becoming depressed, isolated and lonely. For adult adjusters, also, alcohol can remove feelings of inadequacy. The drug, alcohol, gives them a false sense of power. When adjusters drink, they may find themselves aware of heretofore undiscovered options and alternatives. Making decisions becomes easier, and it becomes easier to feel and easier to talk about the real issues. With this new-found power comes increased self-confidence, and in order to maintain these feelings it seems reasonable to have another drink, and another, and yet another. Although such increased drinking does not necessarily mean the adjuster is now also alcoholic, but it does set him or her up to become psychologically dependent on alcohol. Alcohol provides a state of being which feels good; a way of experiencing feelings which can't seem to be experienced except by the use of alcohol.

THE PLACATER

The child who was busy taking care of everyone else's emotional needs -- the warm, sensitive, caring, listening child, the one everyone liked, grows up continuing to take care of others, either personally or occupationally. As a very special friend of mine once said, "Those of us in the helping professions did not gravitate here accidentally. There must have been something wrong with us to be so preoccupied day-in and day-out with the pain of others." Though this statement was said in half-jest, there is an enormous amount of truth in it. For the child who was particularly adept at making others feel comfortable, it becomes only natural to gravitate toward situations which would enable him of her to continue in that manner.

There is something about me that seems to attract sick individuals or simply people with some type of problem.
Della, Social Worker -- Age 38

Fourty-four year old Elaine was raised in a home by two alcoholic parents. When one takes care of others over the years, it is not unusual to arrive at the point Elaine eventually reached. She proceeded to enter into marriages with three different practicing alcoholics. When her third husband was hospitalized for his alcoholism, I asked her during a private session, "While your husband is in this program, what can you do for you so you'll feel better?" Elaine looked away. She began to grimace. She didn't answer my question, nor did she look at me. So, I repeated the question. "Elaine, while your husband is in the hospital for the next three weeks, what can you do for you so you'll feel better?" Again, Elaine looked away but this time not only did she begin to make grimacing gestures with her face, but her shoulders began to twitch and jerk. The jerking was almost spasmodic.

I quickly moved closer and, reaching out to steady her, I said, "Elaine, you don't have to take care of your husband any more! You don't have to take care of him! We are going to take care of him. And you don't have to take care of your two boys tonight. You've already told me they are with friends. It is seven o'clock now. Between seven o'clock and ten o'clock tonight, what are you going to do for you so you will feel better?" There was a pause, but no grimacing, no jerking. Elaine simply said the only thing she could have said. With tears running down her cheeks, she whispered, "I don't know, I don't know."

Of course she didn't know. All her life, the question of what she could do for herself was not a question she could safely explore. Adults who grow up in the roles of placaters, typically go through years of adulthood never seriously considering what they want, rather, they are forever discounting their needs. They have trained themselves to be only concerned with providing for others. The consequence of this behavior is that they never get what they want from life. If we can't ask ourselves what our own wants are, we cannot direct ourselves to obtain them. For the placater, to focus attention to oneself as a child in an alcoholic home was not the key to survival. Survival was concerning oneself with taking away the fears, the sadnesses and the guilts of others. Survival was giving to others. . .one's time, energy, and empathy. And as one 48-year-old woman raised in an alcoholic home, married to a man who was then a recovering alcoholic said, "I am that compulsive giver. I need to become more selfish.

I must quit serving everyone else at my own expense, but I DON'T KNOW HOW. I FEEL SO GUILTY. Giving to others is not bad, but giving at the expense of our own well-being is destructive.

Again, it is relatively easy to understand why these children develop depression as adults. Although they appear to be living their lives the way they want, they still feel apart from others; they feel lonely. They don't have equal relationships with others; and they always give too much and refrain from putting themselves in a position to receive. In personal relationships, placaters seek out other people who are takers, and who refuse to take emotional responsibility in their roles. Placaters look for people who don't want any personal sharing from a friend or loved one. As well, the placaters' partners in life will be people who have also learned not to talk about themselves.

Alcohol performs wonders for many placaters. Drinking helps them talk more freely about themselves, it helps make them to feel more self-worth. The drug alcohol helps placaters to become more assertive; to feel a greater selfishness. It helps them feel and even be angry. If alcohol provides feelings of increased self-worth, an avenue to become more selfish, a part of all placaters will respond positively to the feeling. In fact, they find they need that support to bolster these feelings. Drinking, then, becomes the problem solver. Like adjusters and responsible adult children, many placaters often have a second, a third, a fourth drink -- and before long the psychological trap of alcohol dependency can become a reality.

She was My Mother
Bless Her Soul

i sometimes sit
in the corner
in the dark
and recall my mother
with a brown bottle in her hand
or the sounds of clanking ice at 2 a.m.
she'd call me baby if she wanted another beer
or a slut   if she hadn't had enough
she'd make me cookies on Christmas
before she'd get too drunk
many nights
she would fall asleep on the floor
i'd cover her with a blanket
and put a pillow under her head
i'd awaken in the morning
to the sounds of her
screaming
she wasn't an easy woman to please
most of the time
we didn't get along
sometimes   i miss her
and the loneliness

Jane, adult child

ACTING OUT CHILD

The acting-out children, the ones who were constantly in trouble and caused problems, will continue to find conflicts in early adulthood. As children, and as adults, these persons are not capable of feeling good about themselves. They have been unable to interact with others in acceptable ways, and have been unable to express their own needs or have them met. As children, acting-out children were always aware of their anger, but seldom aware of other feelings. These children usually gravitate toward others with similar personality traits to form a peer group. They seldom respond to any positive role models, and they usually become socially isolated. Should they have been institution-alized in youth, they most often continue this pattern in their adult years.

Acting-out children often begin using and abusing alcohol and other drugs at an early age. Alcohol and drugs are the typical trademarks of rebellious acts for many problematic children. Alcohol provides an avenue which allows them to feel better about themselves, and gives them a false sense of confidence in their abilities. While most acting-out children experiment with alcohol, some quickly become abusers, and soon become alcoholic. These children usually develop alcoholism at earlier ages than other children of alcoholics. The result being that unless there is intervention and treatment which leads to recovery, these young people will die a premature death due to the rapid progression of the disease.

Whether alcoholic or not, upon reaching adulthood, acting-out children find their behavior (or lack or it) has caused major prob-lems which now complicate their adult lives, i.e., lack of high school education, lack of learned skills, inability to control anger (causing the loss of jobs), illegitimate children or youthful mar-riages. It is also typical to find adjusting qualities combined with those of the acting-out child. This combination leads to a feeling of an even greater sense of powerlessness in their lives.

* * * * * *

SUMMARY

Some children may clearly fit into one or more of these four roles. While one child may be an obvious adjuster, another may play both the placating and the responsible roles. Some children exhibit traits of all four roles. A percentage of these children will change and adopt different roles as they grow older. The adjuster may become the placater, the responsible one may become the adjuster. There is no definate pattern to these changes. They are the result of the evolution of the family system.

Whatever roles children adopt, there are gaps in development and growth. Gaps are the emotional and psychological voids which occur as a result of the unpredictable and inconsistent parenting in alcoholic homes. For most children, the gaps are issues related to control, trust, dependency, identification and expression of feelings. These factors will affect the now adult children in: 1) involvement in relationships, particularly intimate ones; as well as lead to 2) depression; and 3) continuance in an alcoholic or otherwise dysfunctional system via marriage, or 4) progression of their own alcoholism.

In the next few chapters, we will discuss how adult children can make changes in their lives. Also, how parents of children still in the home, can affect homelife in a manner that will provide more consistency and predictability for their children.

Delftware

It is time to come in, to
sit at the table cut the meat
pass the potatoes, time to butter
rolls; after that we will eat the pie

Miss Patari yelled it loud from far away
I should have put the paste back in my jar
it dried into a mountain and had to be thrown out.

Come in.
I spell it where I breathe
against the corner of this window, I see you
sitting in the car
behind the windshield where
you tilt your head to swallow.

It is time to come in
and put your medicine away
I don't like so many bottles
when I count them under your bed.

Can we go skating on our blue plate,
the skaters necks are wrapped in scarves
the wind is cold; now dark
I cannot see your face.

                                        Joan, adult child

CHAPTER 5

The Child
Within the Home

CHAPTER FIVE

Even if the alcoholic family member is still a drinking alcoholic, other family members can change the way in which their lives are affected. It is important for the nonalcoholic parent to know life can be better for everyone provided he or she is willing to change some of his or her own behavior patterns and reinforce the basis for new behavior in the children. It is also important for the nonalcoholic parent to be willing to seek outside resources who can aid in re-establishing the necessary direction and who can offer emotional support. Seeking help from strangers may be a very difficult thing to do, but it is more difficult to make positive changes by oneself if outside direction and support is lacking. The nonalcoholic parent should not try to carry the burden of the world on his or her own shoulders, but should be willing to let others help. In seeking outside support, it is important to find qualified professionals with knowledge and understanding of the alcoholic family system. Assistance is equally important not only for the nonalcoholic spouse but for all the children as well. It is not nearly as effective for the spouse alone or only the children alone to receive help -- the entire family must be part of the recovery process. The most accessible resources are programs for the families and friends of the alcoholic offered via outpatient alcohol programs, Al-Anon and Alateen. Typically, when a family member seeks help, the help sought after is for the alcoholic, "Tell me what to do so he will get sober." Agencies will be able to offer guidelines for the alcoholic's treatment, but it is important to remember that whether or not the alcoholic gets sober, the children and the spouse have also been affected by the alcoholism and their problems need to be addressed as well.

As the nonalcoholic spouse and children are involved in Al-Anon, Alateen, and/or other services, the alcoholic might possibly become upset by this involvement. These family members must be encouraged to continue in their own recovery program. Naturally the alcoholic is upset, the boat is being rocked! The nonalcoholic spouse and the children are saying, "We are seeking help because we hurt as a result of your alcoholism. You can get help too, if you want, but we need and want help for ourselves regardless of what you do." Expect the alcoholic person to be threatened. He or she is scared, is feeling guilty and confused. Remember, the truth can only be dealt with when it has been acknowledged. The family is now acknowledging a problem exists, and disclosing that they are feeling hurt because of it.

In most cases, when the alcoholic is faced with the knowledge that family members are seeking outside help, he or she will express verbal anger and then become very sullen and/or passive. Physical violence is not a likely outcome of the alcoholic's knowing the spouse is seeking help unless physical violence has been a past pattern. If violence is a pattern in the household, it is extremely important for the spouse to remove herself or himself and the children from that violent situation and to continue seeking professional help

If the spouse feels it is safe to do so, the alcoholic should be told why the family needs to leave -- because they plan to continue with their program, and will not live in the home where they are physically threatened or hurt. These intentions should only be expressed by the nonalcoholic when there is reason to believe that no further harm will come to any family member. The family's safety should always be the primary concern. (See section on violence for further information.) Again, remember, violence is only apt to occur if it is an already established pattern, and seeking professional help can only benefit the family.

GUIDELINES FOR THE NONALCOHOLIC SPOUSE

It is necessary for children to understand as much about alcoholism as possible. You, the nonalcoholic parent, along with outside, qualified help, should explain and discuss alcoholism with your children.

Concepts which need to be discussed with the children

include: <u>DISEASE CONCEPT</u>. It is advisable to ask your children what they think alcoholism is, and what traits constitute an alcoholic. Children have undoubtedly heard the word "alcoholic" from a friend, or another family member. So often, the word is used judgmentally and negatively. It is important for you to explain alcoholism, as well as to explain why it is necessary for you to discuss the subject. It is vital they understand that the alcoholic family member is sick and suffering from a disease. They should be helped to dispel the misconception that the alcoholic is a "bad" person. When they are made to understand that the alcoholic is a person who cannot stop drinking without help because he or she is physically and psychologically addicted to the drug, alcohol you are beginning to help them view their alcoholic parent in a different light. They need to understand that alcoholism is evident in people who can no longer predict their behavior when drinking; who cannot control their drinking, and whose drinking is causing problems in their lives.

Science has not yet discovered why some people become alcoholic and others do not, nor can we determine alcoholism by the amount a person drinks. Children need not question or attempt to determine why their parents become alcoholic. Many qualified researchers are probing this question for us. But children do need to understand alcoholism is a disease; it is not a problem of lack of self-control. Alcoholism is not a disease caused by a germ or virus as are many other diseases, but it is an illness nonetheless. People do not choose to become alcoholics and all the will power in the world will not cure alcoholism -- the disease makes alcoholics unable to control their drinking and their lives. You and your children, first of all, need to accept that what is occurring in your family is the result of the disease of alcoholism, then proceed with your recovery process.

Telling children they are more prone to become alcoholic because they are the children of alcoholics won't prevent them from developing alcoholism themselves. While this information is valuable to them, it is unrealistic to expect them to choose not to drink because of knowledge alone. Unfortunately, this information will not necessarily be sufficient for them to identify drinking as a problem prior to it becoming a dependency. Parents, concerned other persons, and helping professionals need to recognize children of alcoholics require more than just information. They need psychological, emotional, physical and social intervention, understanding and support.

BLACKOUTS Blackouts are periods of time when the alcoholic, who is conscious and drinking at the time, will have no recall later about the events which occurred during that portion of time. Blackouts are periods of amnesia, varying from minutes to several hours or, for some people, several days. Children and spouses need to understand the alcoholic is not deliberately lying about an event which occurred but because of a physiological reaction caused by the consumption of alcohol they experience these lapses of memory called blackouts.

Some children may suspect their parent, when drinking, actually does not remember a period of time, such as a segment of what happened the night before. Other children who have no knowledge of blackouts experience an even greater sense of confusion and craziness about what happens in the home. Whether or not children recognize when blackouts occur in the alcoholic parent, they need to have some information and an explanation which validates their own experience and allows them to have a better understanding of their parent's denial. This validation also provides an avenue, or permission, to talk about it.

Imagine a Friday night when dad doesn't come home for dinner, and still isn't home when everyone has gone to bed. When he finally does arrive he makes a lot of noise and argues with the 13-year-old he meets in the hallway heading for the bathroom. Dad then proceeds to awaken mom and the two of them argue loudly for several hours in their bedroom. The next day dad only remembers he was drinking with his friends, he was late for dinner and was anticipating his wife would be angry. His recollection stops somewhere in the early evening. He doesn't remember exactly when he got home or if he talked with anyone in the family. The two younger children show some anxiety around dad and are apprehensive of his mood the next morning. The 13-year-old daughter acts abrupt with him. Dad doesn't know why she behaves this way and is fearful of asking, so rather than risk finding out, he treats her with a placating attitude. Mom acts like everything is okay. Because no one talks about the real issues-- dad's behavior the night before, the confusion, the fear and the disappointment. In a family already fragmented more distance and misunderstanding are created.

When children understand blackouts and the fact that dad really may have no recall, they will have the option of checking dad's memory, and pointing out to him what occurred during his blackout. There will be less confusion and fear when the child realizes dad won't be as likely to proceed with the same argument if he has no recall of that argument. Understanding blackouts makes it easier for children to cope with the parent's illness.

PERSONALITY CHANGES are caused by alcoholism. The Jekyll and Hyde phenomenon is certainly witnessed by family members and is not due to craziness, but is in fact, caused by alcoholism. Many people believe when major personality changes occur, they are the result of mental illness; many alcoholics have been labelled and diagnosed as schizophrenic and psychotic personalities. The biographies, "Three Faces of Eve," and "Sybil," tell of women who exhibit major personality changes. . .changes which stem from mental illness. But, for the alcoholic, personality changes and drastic mood swings are due to being alcoholic. The alcohol causes the personality changes. Children need to be made aware that alcohol can cause a total change in personality; that not all people who exhibit such behavior are mentally ill.

The nonalcoholic parent needs to acknowledge the inconsistent patterns of behavior in the home resulting from the alcoholic's behavior and also stemming from their own anger and sometimes irrational responses to that behavior. They need to let the children know they are doing their best to be more predictable. So, hopefully, the only unpredictability will be that of the alcoholic's behavior. Acknowledging that problems in the home are a reality, coupled with renewed attempts to provide consistency, will create much more stability for the children in the home.

BROKEN PROMISES To add stability, the nonalcoholic parent must matter-of-factly acknowledge when promises are broken by the alcoholic. It is important that children know their feelings, such as anger and disappointment, are valid. The nonalcoholic should help the children understand that the alcoholic parent doesn't break promises because of lack of caring or loving. Promises are broken because of the parent's addiction to alcohol. The preoccupation with drinking becomes the alcoholic's number one priority. All else is secondary.

DENIAL When you discuss the alcoholic parent's sickness, blackouts and personality changes, another vital area to discuss is the symptom of denial. Denial occurs when the alcoholic, or enabler, pretends things are different than they really are.

Denial should be presented as a phenomenon family members, as well as the alcoholic, experience. Let the children know certain thoughts and feelings have been denied, i.e., the many times you excused yourself and your alcoholic spouse from a social occasion because you said your spouse was working late, when in reality your spouse was drunk and you were too embarrassed to be seen with him or her. The children too, have denied parts of themselves, i.e., their feelings. Tell them from now on, this family is going to try to be more open and honest about family affairs and about feelings. Denial only harbors resentment, distrust and fear.

ENABLING Nonalcoholic spouses need to teach their children it is okay not to make alibis, or lie, in an attempt to cover up for the alcoholic parent's behavior. They need to model and support nonenabling behavior for the children. Spouses and children often lie to. . .

> clean up after. . .
> make excuses for. . .
> bail out. . .the alcoholic

Family members enable because they feel they must, or because they don't want to risk the unpleasant results of the alcoholic becoming upset or because it simply makes home life easier. There are endless numbers of reasons for enabling behavior. The result of enabling is that the alcoholic does not see and does not address the consequences of drinking behavior. Enabling behavior by family members actually makes it easier for the alcoholic to continue drinking.

RELAPSE is an event which often occurs when the alcoholic is attempting to maintain sobriety. Relapses are not unusual in that they can, and do, occur in most progressive diseases. In a disease such as cancer, there are times when the cancer appears to be "arrested," it is not progressing. Then, it begins its process again, and the cancer victim is said to have had a relapse. When someone has pneumonia and recovers, often they suffer a relapse and return to being sick. A definition of relapse was most eloquently stated by a 9-year-old whose mother was alcoholic.

> *A relapse is when you stop drinking and then you start again. It's like when you have a cold and you think it is gone. Then you go out in the rain and your cold comes back.*
>
> *Melody, Age 9*

Relapse is a term which needs to be discussed if a parent attempts to get sober. Many parents ask "why worry the child?" not realizing the child is already worried. The child's worries are validated and less overwhelming if this concern is discussed.

However, family members need to go about their daily activities without being preoccupied with the possibility of relapse. In discussing relapse, it is necessary for children to understand they don't cause relapses. Even if it appears dad's relapse was precipitated by the 16-year-old son wrecking the family car, dad must learn to cope with such problems, or uncomfortable feelings, without reaching for alcohol. The alcoholic is not guilty for having the disease, but is responsible for the decision to drink again. There is much the alcoholic needs to learn to do in order to prevent relapse, and other family members can best understand this through their own involvement in a recovery program.

Children are not immune from the effects of alcoholism, they live with it, they need to understand it. I believe children of all ages can comprehend these concepts pertaining to alcoholism if the concepts are explained in language the children understand. It is important for children to have access to literature which will reinforce healthy messages. Parents need to be willing to talk openly about these concepts. Together, parents and children will have the information to understand and better cope with alcoholism and the problems the disease creates.

* * * * * *

"MY DADDY"

I woke up one morning and he was gone
he was gone my Daddy
and he would never be home again
he was gone my Daddy
the one who always showed his love
the one who always understood, when
she never would!
the one who always brushed my hair,
combed and put ribbons in my hair
he was the one who picked me up
when I fell and skinned my knee
Oh my daddy, my daddy
I still remember all the things he taught
me - - - but he was gone.
and I was too young to understand
she said they just didn't get along - - -
I hardly ever saw him, my daddy who
was always there, my daddy who always cared.
It seemed he just didn't have time for me.
But that was also ten years age and I think
now I understand- - -But there's still one question
that remains. And that's - - - - - - - - - -
Why Oh Lord, did this have to happen to me?????
Why did my daddy have to go, and leave me all alone- - -
She says he's alcoholic, a person who has a disease
and needs help. . . .But can only get it if he
wants it.
He must admit to himself that he is sick and needs
help. . . .She knows all this now and I do too. . .
Now its to late, he's already gone. . .
He's remarried now and he has a new little princess
who he brushes, combs, and puts ribbons in her hair
But Lord this is so unfair!!!
He is my daddy and he needs help!!!
But I feel so helpless Lord because it seems he still
doesn't have time for me. I Love My Daddy, whom I
hardly ever see. And even more when I think about
how much he must Love Me- - - - -MY DADDY

Renee, age 16

FEELINGS

When working with children of alcoholics, I often address them in terms of their losses, specifically losses which occur as a result of parents not being there for them on a consistent basis. The loss of attention occurs because of the alcoholic's preoccupation with alcohol, and the co-alcoholic's preoccupation with the alcoholic. When children experience a loss, they enter a grief process, one which is similar to the grief processes other people experience when they lose a loved one due to death, or when a loved one becomes incapacitated because of a serious illness. The same kind of grief occurs when a person loses a limb, or other part of the body.

The first state of the grief process is disbelief, or denying the loss has really happened. In essence, the disbelief may be natures way of helping a person through this stage by deadening the pain, by giving a person time to absorb the facts. Unfortunately, with alcoholism, this grief process is much slower; it occurs over a much longer time and is much more subtle than the grief experienced due to losing someone through death.

With alcoholism, as time passes and the truth becomes more evident, the victim's family begins to experience the terror. . .the terror of the reality that a loved one is an alcoholic. Usually, the next emotion following the terror is anger. "If you (the alcoholic) really love me, how can you be like this?" The family members often feel guilt. Each family member believes, that in some way, they are responsible. A son believes, "Maybe if I hadn't talked back, dad wouldn't drink so much, or be so angry all the time." A wife believes, "If I were a better wife, my husband wouldn't be sick." A husband believes, "Maybe if I had been home more. . .," etc. Bargaining is practiced by family members eliciting promises from the drinker to control or stop the drinking; at other times bargaining is self-imposed, "If I behave this way, maybe mom will respond another way." For many children the bargaining is through prayer, "Please God, keep my mom and dad together. Don't let them fight so much. I promise I will be real good." Finally family members feel desperation and despair.

They each feel alone with the problem. They feel all these terrible things are unique in their lives, that no one else could possibly understand their pain. They despair that there are no answers or solutions to the guilt they carry. This process and these feelings are common to all persons affected by the alcoholism.

Families who try to run away from their feelings suffer longer. Often, they never recover from their grief, and it becomes a long lasting depression. Families who face their loss, and the related feelings, accept the stages of grief human beings seem to need to go through. These families will become stronger and will be able to begin growing, living full and satisfying lives.

In alcoholic families, everyone suffers, and everyone suffers very much alone. Children often suffer from loneliness, fear, anger and a multitude of other feelings which they have no way of understanding. Furthermore they do not have the ability to express this lack of understanding. I believe a child can survive a family crisis as long as he or she is told the truth and allowed to share the natural sequence of feelings people experience when they suffer.

It is important for the nonalcoholic to talk with the children about these feelings and explain that these feelings are perfectly normal. Although the nonalcoholic may help the children understand alcoholism, intellectual understanding will not erase the multitude of intense feelings they experience. Children need to be able to say, "I was so embarrassed. I know she is sick, but she still embarrasses me, and it hurts!" Or, "I'm sad because mom is like she is. But, I'm also really angry, and I don't understand why she won't go for help!" All of these feelings are valid. Children can understand and feel at the same time. They need to know others will validate and listen to their feelings. The nonalcoholic parent, along with outside resources, can fill this necessary validating role.

Crying

Crying is a natural release for emotions. Children and spouses both, need to cry. Crying is difficult for many people, but people in alcoholic homes usually do one of two things: 1) They learn how not to cry; or 2) They cry alone, very silently.

EVERY NIGHT BEFORE DINNER WHEN DADDY GETS HOME, MOMMY AND DADDY FIGHT. DADDY SAYS MOMMY SHOULDN'T HAVE ANOTER GLASS OF SHERRY.
MOMMY SAYS SHE'S ONLY HAD 2!

I WAIT AND CRY IN THE HALL. I DON'T WANT THEM TO SEE ME.

Tracy, 17

Before a child can cry and feel okay about it, the child needs to be given healthy messages regarding crying: "It's okay to cry, it's normal." "It will make you feel better." Other messages, such as, "Boys don't cry," "Boys shouldn't cry," "Don't be a crybaby," need to be countered. Children also need models who can demonstrate that crying is not weak or shameful. They need you, the sober parent, to be honest about yourself. You may have to confide in the children that you have been pretending you don't hurt. You may have to tell them you really do hurt and, at times, you too, cry. Tell them you feel awkward about sharing this secret with them, but when you do share, you feel closer to them-- and you feel better. Aside from giving permission to cry, you need to be supportive of their sharing their feelings with others. Ask your children who they could tell about the times when they cried? Who do they trust enough to confide in? Who in the family do they trust to ask for comfort at such times? This can be a very valuable family discussion.

I once worked with a brother and sister, 6-year-old Chuck, and his 9-year-old sister, Melody. Chuck was very open about not trusting his mother, and about his helplessness regarding her drinking. He talked about worrying a lot and, at times, he cried when he talked. Melody would tell him to shut-up. She would talk louder when he was speaking and would call him a cry baby. She was prepared to do just about anything she could to keep Chuck from talking and showing his feelings. Though there was only three years difference in their ages, Chuck and Melody were in different stages of denial. It is important for a parent to be aware of there varying stages of denial among children, and how children interfere with, or are supportive of, each other's expressions of feelings. One child may be more open to expression of tears, while another is obviously angry; still another child appears simply to be nonfeeling. All children need to have access to all of their feelings, and have healthy avenues of expression.

Fearful

Fear is a natural emotion all children experience. It is, unfortunately, normal for a child to be acutely fearful in an alcoholic home. Whether or not children express specific fears, parents, family and friends need to validate that, at times, it is quite reasonable to be afraid. Many times, nothing can be done about feelings such as fear, other than helping children talk about them. Expressing feelings develops a closeness between a parent and children, and is helpful in decreasing the children's feelings of being overwhelmed by emotions they are keeping inside. Emotions become so much more powerful when they are not outwardly expressed, secrets can cause a great deal more pain than is necessary.

A parent's drinking results in a lot of tension in the home, and it's important to approach children individually and acknowledge each of their fears. The non alcoholic parent should tell them that alcoholism causes people to act in ways which are scary. Caution! Don't ask them if they are okay. They hear that as a leading question which tells them you want them to say "yes." Instead, ask them how they feel about the family's situation.

Listen and validate their feelings.

Another positive result of talking about feelings is that problems can be solved. Suppose this coming Friday, Sally has an important mother-daughter function, and mom's attendance is dependent on whether or not she drinks that day. Though Sally has not approached her father with an expression of fear, the father can approach Sally saying, "I know you function is on Friday, and I'm sure it is important to you. Your mother told me about it herself last night. You're probably concerned as to whether or not she'll really attend." At that point, the parent should stop and listen. Give Sally a chance to respond. It is very appropriate to problem-solve with her. It's up to the sober parent, to engage Sally in mutual problem solving, "Have you thought about what you'll do if she is drinking then?" Once again, listen. Then offer possibilities should she need such guidance. Certainly, the possibilities include: 1) Sally would not go; 2) she would go alone; 3) she would ask another person to attend in lieu of her mother; or 4) she would go with a friend and her friend's mother. It is important Sally not isolate herself as a result of her mother's drinking and that she continue with her plans as close to the original idea as possible. It is healthy to encourage the child to attend the function, and to use an alternative support system. Problem-solving is more likely to occur when feelings are discussed, both before and after an event which could be marred due to someone's drinking.

Anger

Anger is a normal feeling. Everyone experiences it. For the majority of children of alcoholics, I found this to be the feeling they were most reticent to share. It is extremely important for children to become aware of their frustrations and angers, and then find ways to express these frustrations. Children's anger is only problematic when it has been stored, and when appropriate ways of expression have not been introduced to the children. Parents need to assess their own ability to identify and express feelings, and embark on healthier ways of expressing those feelings as they teach them to their children.

Parents should ask themselves: "What do I do with my anger?" "What do my children do?" Whether or not you think you know, ask them anyway. Ask them what happens when family members get angry. In doing this, you are asking them how they perceive the way anger is expressed at home. Their responses will guide you in determining what needs to be addressed; i.e., when 9-year-old Mike was asked what people in his family do with anger, he said, "Dad leaves the house. Mom drinks. Tommy goes outside. I'm not really angry. Mike was a very overweight young boy, and his description demonstrated how he had copied his mother's pattern for coping with anger, while his brother copied his father's pattern. Two family members leave their anger behind, and two drink or eat at it. None of them found a healthy way of coping with anger.

Children need to know their anger will not cause them to lose their parent's love. For so many people, expressing anger has come to mean, "If I show you I'm angry with you, you will withdraw your love." Children need to know what limits are placed on the expression of anger, and what is perceived by others as appropriate responses to situations.

Children need to know their hurts and angers are very important and should not be discounted. Many times, children discount problems in their own lives because they believe problems taking place within the family structure take precedence over any personal conflicts occuring outside the home. "Who am I to talk about how angry I became at school today, there is already enough tension at home." The messages learned are: 1) what happened to me at school is not important; 2) the feelings I have throughout the day at school are not important; 3) I am not important. It bears repeating, nonalcoholic parents raising children in a drinking, alcoholic environment need outside resources to help. These outside resources; i.e., a school counselor, or an Alateen meeting, can help validate the expression of feelings, whether big or small.

Guilt

Kids assume they have power to affect everything when, in

truth, they have very little power in an alcoholic environment. "All dad ever hollered about was us kids, so I assumed we had to be making him drink." Children need to know they do not cause alcoholism, and it is not their behavior which causes a parent to continue drinking alcoholically. Children need to be reassured even if they behave in a way which upsets a parent, that their parent has many choices other than drinking to handle the situation. Remind them no one is responsible for the alcoholic's actions, save the alcoholic, and their (the children's) actions cannot cause alcoholism. Reaffirm the illness concept. Acknowledge the children's feelings of helplessness, but don't let them continue creating guilt from the lack of power they experience. Help them, once again, to see what they are doing is positive; i.e., not enabling, not being judgmental, but being honest with the alcoholic parent when sober, etc.

Typically, when children feel guilty, they are feeling many other feelings which also need to be acknowledged. Elizabeth, age 11, looked up at me during a therapy session and blurted out, "But I don't love my mom." She waited for me to validate or chastise her for feeling this way. I responded with, "It hurts, doesn't it Elizabeth? It's okay if you don't feel like you love mom. I'm sure a lot has happened to make you feel that way. It's really okay." I then went on to talk about love and hate, conflicting feelings, and how people feel guilty when they think they are supposed to feel one way, but actually feel another. Children may feel hate, dislike, a numbness toward, or simply feel they don't love their parents. They then feel guilty for experiencing these thoughts. Children not only feel guilt because they think they are the cause of the problem, or because they cannot remedy the problem, but they also feel guilty for having conflicting feelings of love and hate for the alcoholic, or nonalcoholic, parent.

Kids learn early in childhood that they are expected to love and respect their parents. Father Joseph Martin, a renowned educator and counselor in the field of alcoholism, believes practicing alcoholics are incapable of loving anyone, including themselves. An alcoholic whose number 1 priority is to drink, is incapable of acting in ways which demonstrates or accepts love.

Love consists of mutual respect, trust and sharing, all the characteristics an alcoholic loses for himself and for others. The inability of the alcoholic to love and accept love is both frustrating and confusing for the children. It is also understandable for children not to love their parent, they may need the parent, but need by itself is not love.

* * * * * *

Children have to be helped to understand that feelings are transitory. . .feelings change. One may feel intense hatred for a person, then, at another time, feel empathy for that same person. One may experience great tenderness toward a person now, and become enraged with the same person a few hours later. Feelings change, and children will not be "stuck" with a feeling forever. Most children do not realize this by themselves; it must be explained to them in terms they can understand.

Children need to know it is possible to experience more than one feeling at a time. Sadness and anger can be felt together, as can happiness and sadness, fear and anxiety, love and hate. There are numerous combinations. What's important is that the adult be accepting of the child's feelings, even if the child says, "I don't love mom. I hate her." If adults can accept and validate childrens' feelings of intense dislike, as well as anger, fear and disappointment, then adults can also help children not to live lives of guilt for having these feelings. We can help children work through these feelings and, hopefully, acquire a more positive acceptance of themselves.

Though love was discussed relative to guilt, it is vital to remember most children do love their parents, and love will usually withstand a lot of inconsistent, even trauma inducing, parenting. Remember love relates to the experiences shared prior to the onset of alcoholism, as well as to the sober moments shared. Alcoholic parents are not drunk all the time, in fact, many never appear drunk (they are just never sober). Alcoholism is a process, the onset of which most often begins in a person's mid-20s and early 30s. This indicates that most parents begin raising their children in nonalcoholic years or early alcoholic years. When a person is in the early stages of alcoholism their behavior may not be consistently disruptive to the family. The same is true regarding love for the nonalcoholic parent. While nonalcoholic parents over time become depressed, angry, rigid, or absent, this behavior was not typical of them in the early stages. Nonalcoholic parents too, were more consistent with their children and provided more quality time for them. So children often did learn to love their parents in a once healthier environment.

Also remember while we cannot make children love their parents, we can help them not to hate. It is easier for children not to "get stuck" in hate if we can provide more consistency in their lives as well as educating them to better understand alcoholism and its' effects on the alcoholic and on the entire family structure.

Children usually learn about feelings and what to do with them by modeling adults. The more healthy role models that are available, the greater their ability to adopt that healthy behavior and utilize positive avenues of expression. The more isolated the alcoholic family becomes, the fewer options children have to learn from healthy adults. Children need access to healthy role models.

Parents will not be able to attend to each and every feeling their children experience. But, if they consistently offer healthy messages and validations, and model ways to cope with feelings, the children won't need constant support for every feeling they experience.

MANIPULATIVENESS

Some children, particularly adolescents, recognize they have the power to manipulate the alcoholic during spells of personality changes, remorse and blackouts. Children quickly learn they have power over certain situations in their lives, and use this knowledge to their own advantage. 'I know dad will let me out Saturday night, no questions asked, after he's been drinking. So, I'll wait until late Friday night to ask. If I ask earlier, he'll be more

sober and he'll ask me twenty questions about what I am doing."
Or, "Ask dad for your allowance when he's drinking, and he'll
give you $20 instead of $5." The best way to handle children
taking advantage during such times is to seriously discuss the
parent's alcoholism with them. Explain the sickness to them and
why they are not to prey on it. The nonalcoholic parent will need
to demonstrate via actions that they are taking a greater role in
parenting, will set rules and see that situations are handled fairly.

Be aware that children will not only manipulate the alcoholic,
but will use similar tactics on the co-alcoholic parent. Recognize
also that the co-alcoholics have developed feelings of guilt
because they know the children suffer from lack of proper attention. (The lack of attention stems from the alcoholic because of
the obsession with drinking; and this same lack of attention is
felt from the co-alcoholic because his or her attention is directed
to the alcoholic and the problems resulting from the drinking.)
Children are children, and their manipulativeness can be expected as a normal part of their growing up process, but if
children are dealt with consistently and fairly, their
manipulativeness can be reduced to a reasonable level.

PROTECTION

Carrie, age 6, came to her fifth children's group with her older
brother, Tony, age 8, and proposed this problem: both children
told me their dad had returned to drinking since he left the
alcoholism treatment program five weeks earlier. Because they
did not live with their dad, and saw him only on weekends, his
drinking was not strongly interfering with the child-parent relationship. They explained that even though dad was drinking, he
wasn't getting drunk nor was he causing any problems. During
this particular meeting, Carrie told us her dad promised to take
her to Disneyland next weekend. She had been to Disneyland the
year before and really liked it. Tony wouldn't be going along
because he was taking a weekend trip with their mother. While
Carrie wanted to go to Disneyland, she was scared her father
would drink, ruining the trip.

Carrie loved her dad and wanted to be with him. And, she wanted to go to Disneyland--but she was also frightened. She was scared of being embarrassed should her father drink, and she feared his ability to drive safely on the one and one-half hour trip home. On the other hand, she felt a need to protect her father and didn't want to hurt his feelings by telling him he frightens her. Carrie further believes that if she told her father why she is afraid, he would stop taking her places, and would not want to see her at all.

Carrie didn't want to share her fears with her mother, because her mother might not let her go to Disneyland at all, and Carrie knew she couldn't go on the weekend trip with mom and Tony. Finally, she said, "It's all so complicated. Besides, maybe dad won't drink anyway." Carrie was very concerned and exasperated about her dilemma which clearly demonstrated that her father's return to drinking was causing considerable problems for her.

In the same group, Trisha, age 11, who goes to her dad's house on weekends told us, "Dad goes out in the evenings and drinks; he stays out real late!" Trisha said she stays alone during these evenings, alone, worrying about her dad, and crying a lot. Trisha feels she can't make her dad stay home, yet she doesn't want to tell her mother, who may not let her spend weekends at her father's.

While these are certainly not the most severe problems encountered by young children, they are representative of the dilemmas children usually face in trying to resolve problems by themselves.

For both Trisha and Carrie, there are not any clear-cut satisfactory answers for such problems. But, all children need an adult, preferably a parent to: 1) offer them guidance, 2) protect them, and 3) give them permission to protect themselves.

Offer children these basic messages: 1) the alcoholic parent is sick and not always able to make the best decisions, and 2) it is important and permissable to ask others for help. When children have been briefed on possible situations, given positive messages about themselves, and when they believe they will be supported by an adult they will usually choose better options.

Parents can explore possible courses of action prior to a problem occurring. Children can better handle problems and protect themselves, if necessary, if they have the time to discuss and think over potential situations. It is even more helpful if these discussions include the alcoholic parent, or if the alcoholic parent is told the children have been given instructions and/or permission to protect themselves. Be sure the alcoholic is sober when brought into these discussions!

I suggest these options be covered during a family gathering where everyone can write down situations they are fearful of addressing, or situations they have already addressed, but want to explore further. Remember, the alcoholic won't be particularly receptive to this idea, but it needs to be done nonetheless.

When having periodic family meetings to discuss such situations, it is important that each participant be given the opportunity to talk about past situations without fear of others' judgments. For this gathering to be successful, it should to be conducted by a caring adult who understands alcoholism. If the co-alcoholic is not participating in a recovery process, through Al-Anon and/or counseling, this format is not likely to work. This occasion should not be used to "dump" on the alcoholic; but rather, to talk about how to handle situations which pose problems. It is a meeting where children can participate and walk away with workable options.

Page 89 is an example of a form which may be very helpful in conducting a family discussion. Provide several for each family member. Let each keep his or her own copy, and have extras for other problems they may attempt to solve on their own, or for the next family meeting.

Each member of the family needs to make a personal list of "What ifs"--posing actual or potential problems. The possibilities which follow are the results of mutual talking and problem solving with family groups. Talk with the children about how they can protect themselves how to avoid dangerous or vulnerable positions.

PROBLEM SOLVING

Situations   **Possibilities**

WHAT IF. . .

                      1 .

                      2 .

                      3 .

WHAT IF. . .

                      1 .

                      2 .

                      3 .

WHAT IF. . .

                      1 .

                      2 .

                      3 .

PROBLEM SOLVING

Situations	Possibilities
Child's "WHAT IF"...	
Dad and I are planning to go to a ball game Saturday afternoon, but he begins drinking early that morning.	1. Don't go with dad, anywhere, once he has already started to drink.
	or
	2. Don't go with dad anywhere once he has been drinking for a couple of hours.
	I can tell him:
	a. I changed my mind, that's all;
	b. Mom said I couldn't go;
	c. The family agreement says not to go once he has been drinking.

The role of the nonalcoholic adult during the problem solving sessions is twofold: 1) to provide guidance and offer suggestions so children realize they <u>do</u> have alternative choices; 2) to reassure children that they will have support in these choices, and that their choices will not be discounted, nor will children be punished for their feelings.

PROBLEM SOLVING (continued)

Situations	Possibilities

Child's "WHAT IF". . .

I am with dad, 40 minutes from home, and his driving is scaring me. He doesn't seem drunk but he has had at least 6 beers in the last two hours.

1. If I am in the car and dad is driving, tell him his driving scares me and ask him to slow down, or pull over.

   (This request is only likely to work if dad has been forewarned of it. It may not be an option if dad is more likely to become angry.)

2. If he pulls the car over, or if I ask him to pull the car over, I will call the other parent or friend (a person already designated and who has agreed to help when available). Someone will come to pick me up.

While these possibilities are not necessarily always workable, children need to know they are not expected to stay in a situation which frightens them, and if they choose alternatives, other caring adults will support their actions.

It is important to remember these are merely options, not necessarily suggestions or recommendations for your family members. Each family unit knows its own situations best. What is important here is the process of identifying potential and actual problems, and then seeking viable options.

Also, remember children do want to spend time and share experiences with their parents. Not all time children spend with an alcoholic parent is bad or trauma-causing; there can be wonderfully pleasant times. Children do not need to be isolated from an alcoholic parent, nor will they be "hurt" because they witness isolated incidents of a parent's drinking, or being intoxicated. As well, it is important to remember children will feel deprived if they lose the option of spending time with the alcoholic. Sometimes children will risk riding with dad while he is drunk because they want to go somewhere important to them, i.e., the department store, a friend's house, the ballgame, etc. They may risk a potentially embarassing situation in inviting friends home to maintain friendships, or risk, inviting the alcoholic parent to a school fucntion to show their pride in that parent.

In Trisha's and Carrie's cases, they both eventually decided they wanted to go with their fathers. We adults need to understand the children's need and love for their parent. Remember, a valuable and loving relationship can be possible, even with an alcoholic parent.

PROBLEM SOLVING (continued)

Situations	Possibilities

Carrie's "WHAT IF". . .

Carrie's problem-- fear that dad will go to Disneyland and drink. Fear of embarassment, and dad's drunken driving. But she decides she will go.

1 . Tell dad about concerns prior to going, ask him to try not to drink.
2 . Ask dad to take a specific adult friend (one you know and suggest) for protection.

Trisha's "WHAT IF". . .

Trisha decides for herself she wants to go to dad's each weekend, but doesn't want to be alone, and feel bad. She asks him to stay home on evenings, but that hasn't worked.

1 . Tell dad I love him and want him to stay with me since I only see him on weekends.
2 . Take games with me knowing I will probably be alone at night.
3 . Tell dad I want to have a friend spend nights with me if he is going to go out.

Adult family members have "WHAT IF'S", as well.

Parent's "WHAT IF". . .

What if I fear fire since the alcoholic smokes while severely intoxicated; she has burned holes in the furniture.

1 . Get fire alarm for house.
2 . Identify escape routes.
3 . Have fire drill.
4 . If I am away (nonalcoholic parent), provide another adult to stay or have children stay at another home.
(Do not allow children to sit all night in fear.)

If the alcoholic is not in the meeting when the problem solving possibilities are discussed, it can be helpful to tell the alcoholic about the family's plan of action. In the last example, as escape routes are identified and a fire alarm is purchased, be sure the alcoholic knows his or her behavior (as a result of alcoholism) is perceived as a major threat to the family's safety.

PROBLEM SOLVING (Continued)

Situations	Possibilities

Adult child's "WHAT IF". . .

Don't want to go to parents' for Christmas due to mom's usual drunkenness at this time. Don't want dad to be alone, yet don't want children to experience another Christmas with drunk grandparents.	1. Invite dad to come alone for the Christmas gathering, and tell him why.
	2. Go for limited time, 2 hours vs. all day.
	3. Extend an invitation to mom to come to your house. She knows your rule, "No Drinking."

If options are not found which will help the family feel safer during a particular situation, ask a professional alcoholism counselor for suggestions.

Obviously, children are more likely to use any option if they know they will be supported and positive response from another adult will follow. This "family discussion" approach is a major step which will begin breaking down the alcoholic's denial process, and will eliminate the rules of "not talking", "not feeling" and "not trusting".

RESHAPING ROLES -- FOR THE YOUNG CHILD

As described in Chapter 4, the "Progression of Roles," whichever roles children adopt, (responsible, adjusting, placating or acting out) lead them to have "gaps." Gaps are psychological voids which result from inconsistent parenting and the lack of appropriate and emotional support. These voids are integrated into the children's social development, and create major problems for these children in adulthood. The gaps include not learning to relax, not knowing how to rely on others, not knowing how to follow, or not knowing how to lead, never allowing one's own needs to be met, and many other undeveloped coping mechanisms. Not only will these gaps create living problems but they may result in the predisposition of the children to marry and/or become alcoholic themselves. These gaps and voids are those which most often predispose children to experience emotional problems.

When giving the children an understanding of alcoholism through talking about the real issues, and teaching them to identify and express feelings while establishing healthy support networks, there is also a specific need to focus on reshaping roles.

There are obvious benefits in learning a sense of responsibility, adjusting and placating; yet, in this process gaps are created because children have not acquired a sense of emotional balance. They adopt the roles I've described out of a severe need, a sense of survival, so that they may bring about consistency to an extremely chaotic and unpredictable family system. So, while you the nonalcoholic parent should not seek to take away the positive aspects of any role, you will need to help children achieve a better sense of balance in certain areas. In essence, you need to fill the gaps. You must take time to develop an environment in which the children can learn the social skills their natural survival techniques are not allowing them to learn.

Reshaping of roles generally means you must change your expectations of your children's behaviors and also change your behavior toward the children. Instead of becoming immediately frustrated when your 8-year-old acts 8 years of age and insisting she act like a little adult, allow her to display some of that normal 8-year-old behavior. This will require more patience on the parent's part. When your placating child reaches out to placate one more time, rather than applaud him, let him know you appreciate his thoughtfulness, but you want to be alone, and you are going to call an adult friend to talk.

As you assist in reshaping roles, you may experience resistance from the children in a variety of ways. Children may exhibit confusion, depression, withdrawal or anger. Remember, change in any system, even when that change is positive such as suggested here, is often met with resistance. Be aware that your children will feel awkward about making changes, but these feelings are natural and are to be expected.

You can expect a certain amount of rebellion from a 10-year-old who has been busy playing "mom" and "little adult" when you suggest she try to play hopscotch and giggle with her friends--behavior which has been totally out of her realm of reality.

A similar rebellion will come from the adjusting child when you ask him to share his anger or hurt. For this son, who managed to stare at the television all the while dad was drunkenly ranting and raving, and who showed no signs of being affected, to share feelings now seems far beyond his present capabilities.

For the placating child, who has been taking care of everyone else's feelings, to become more selfish about her own feelings is a difficult task. Being selfish does not give her the satisfaction she felt in taking care of others. She has not learned to feel good about herself when she is away from her charges. This becomes a very frightening time of adjustment for her.

Reshaping roles will be difficult whether or not the drinking has stopped. Role reshaping must be done slowly, and it is more effective when several adults are involved in the process. Tell grandparents, extended family, neighbors and school personnel how they can be helpful to the children.

In reshaping roles, I am not suggesting you take a responsible child and make him irresponsible, or an adjusting child and make her inflexible, or a placating child and make him totally egocentric. I am suggesting these children learn a balance of roles, and experience a sense of choice when they respond to different situations.

It is important for all children to develop a sense of choice about where this responsibility lies. You, the parent, need to help all your children accept certain responsibilities for themselves, and to reward them verbally for their accomplishments. While some children will take on more responsibility than others, it is very important for you not to allow one child to take on the surrogate or strong parenting role for the other children. For that overly responsible child, this may mean that you relieve him of the necessity to do certain "responsible" things, at the same time being supportive of other "fun" activities appropriate for a child his age. You may find yourself saying to Tom, "Mrs. Brown from next door will be here when your sister comes home from school today, so if you want, you can stay after school for about 45 minutes and play." Your changing of roles may mean you are spreading the areas of responsibility and it may mean you are providing others to share the responsible role the child previously held alone. Spreading the responsibility may mean providing a babysitter even through your 10-year-old is extremely responsible and nearly as capable as the 15-year-old you hire to babysit. It could mean that you get up 20 minutes early in the morning and prepare a casserole. This makes you, the adult, responsible for dinner, and not your 12-year-old. Children need your support and encouragement to make friends and to be involved in after-school play activities. Applaud and encourage them to take time out to play and laugh.

Be careful not to de-emphasize the importance of responsibility with overly responsible children. Instead, emphasize parts of their characters they have not yet actualized -- their spontaneity, their playfulness, their ability to lean on someone, their ability to recognize that they are not compelled to have all the answers. Responsible children need to be praised and have their deeds acknowledged, not only when they are doing their best and acting as strong leaders, but when other endeavors take them out of the leadership role, such as playing on a team without being the captain. Remember, while these children demonstrate leadership qualities, this personality characteristic will only be healthy when it is not adopted as a matter of survival. Reinforce the children's natural need to share with, and lean on, others when they have to make decisions and work on projects. Let them know you are the parent, and although they are bright and accomplished youngsters, they are still just that -- youngsters. People of all ages need help, advice and guidance at some points in their lives; these messages are best transmitted when both your words and your actions coincide.

With children who are not overly responsible, you should encourage them to take risks and make decisions for themselves. They need to learn to trust their own decision-making processes. They need to find, when they do make a decision, you really will follow through and support them. Start with situations which are the least threatening and have the fewest possible negative consequences -- what television show to watch, what to have for dinner, how to handle a project. These children must learn to feel good about themselves because of their own accomplishments and their own decisions, not because they seek your approval. Remember, the placating child will gladly make a decision if that is what is necessary to obtain your approval. Parental approval is not the proper goal, however. The goal is to instill in children the ability to make their own healthy decisions, to learn organizational skills and to know how to problem solve.

As you teach the adjusting and placating children a sense of leadership, you will be teaching the responsible children some adjusting qualities. They will most likely learn to adjust only when they find others are capable and willing to provide direction for them. Until the willingness is demonstrated by others responsible children won't trust relinquishing control.

As you help children identify and share feelings, you will need to spend more time with the placating child reinforcing the fact that he or she is not responsible for another's feelings. For instance, when you were crying because your husband was verbally abusive, let your child know it hurt your feelings, and yes, you are sad, but the child is not responsible for your sadness. Share with your child that you are okay, but you've just had your feelings hurt.

Placating children need to learn to play, as do other children who take on adult roles. These children need a lot of reinforcement from you in order to learn it is okay to have their own needs met. Placating children become more stable when they know others are aware of, and sensitive to, the feelings in the home, and that those feelings are being denied.

For the acting-out child, recognize that this child is displaying unacceptable behavior because of: 1) family problems, 2) inability to have needs met, and 3) lack of knowledge as to how to let others know what is wanted. Acting-out children, many times, were initially responsible and sensitive to others but found it brought them no satisfaction. The consequences became rebellion -- rebellion used to ward off pain. Many acting-out children have the ability to lead and can respond sensitively to others when in the right environment. These children must learn new productive outlets for anger; these children need validation and consistency in their lives. Quite often acting-out children need to be counseled by a helping professional. The professional should be a person experienced in dealing with both alcoholic families and adolescents. Ideally, the entire family will be counseled. Acting-out children need to learn to express fears, disappointments and failures, as well as successes, in a loving, safe environment; that is, a good family therapy setting.

THE NONDRINKING ALCOHOLIC HOME

Much of what I have said about roles applies also to children of alcoholics even though the alcoholic may now be sober, or is no longer living with the family due to separation, divorce or death. Patterns don't stop because drinking stops. Children, by themselves, do not recognize the need for change. It is so very typical for people to believe if the drinking stops, or if the drinker leaves the family, that everything will be back to normal. Unfortunately, that is not the case.

I'm reminded of a 19-year-old who told me she continues to lie about insignificant events. She developed this pattern in an effort to bring stability to a very violent alcoholic home. When she told me this, the violence and the alcoholic parent had been out of the home for three years (due to divorce). She said she was not aware of her pattern of lying until she was confronted with the behavior -- three years after the alcoholic parent had left the family. One reason family members do not change their ways after the alcoholic has left is because they seldom realize they have been adversely affected.

A 43-year-old recovering alcoholic told me that even after six years of sobriety, he had not once talked to his children about his alcoholism, or the effects it had on the family. He explained he now feels close to his children (two adult children in their early 20's, and a 14-year-old), yet regrets that many things have been left unsaid. He recognizes the negative impact his alcoholism had on the family, but he doesn't know how to approach his children about these problems carried over from the past.

It definitely is awkward, after any number of years, to bring up these sensitive issues. However, in the long run, if these problems are not addressed, they become more and more difficult to solve. This closeting of feelings creates a distance and perpetuates a lack of communication among family members. The ability to deny is likely to continue if children are not able to talk about their feelings or refer to past events in their lives. The ability to deny is a given, unless the family makes a specific effort to alter old family laws and roles. Family members need not have family secrets. When the family has reunited as a result of a recovery process, its members can become even closer, and family life can become even better as long as past and present problems are dealt with in an open and honest manner.

Should family members be involved in a recovery process prior to the alcoholic's sobriety, it is important that they continue in the recovery program even after their alcoholic gets sober. It has taken many years to develop a denial system. While family members may have worked through some of their denial by the time the alcoholic seeks help, it is very natural for them to stop their therapy and revert to old ideas, thinking once the alcoholic does seek treatment that the worst is behind them. Family members, as well as the alcoholic, have been perfecting their denial systems for years and, while it may not take equally as many years to undo that system, the recovery process is still a lengthy one.

I was working with a 12-year-old boy at the time his father was first getting sober. We had worked rather quickly through the denial system, but after his father left the treatment facility and returned home, Mike came back to group and said, "Everything is just really wonderful." He was smiling and had absolutely no problem in the world! I knew his father had been a drinking alcoholic all of Mike's life. Mike believed because dad was now sober, dad was going to wake up, and no longer anesthesized, dad was going to "discover" his 12-year-old son -- a boy he knew very little about. I knew Mike's life just couldn't remain all roses. I was also hearing from Mike's mother that he was having a difficult time in school. One day, I finally confronted Mike, "Mike, things aren't fine, are they?" "Oh yeah, they are just fine," he responded. I said, "No, Mike, things are not just fine. Things are often not good even though a parent gets sober." Finally, Mike said to me, (through the form of a picture), "I have a hard time understanding why my dad goes to those meetings every night, and why he is not home." Mike had a lot of expectations, many of which were fantasies, about how he and his father were going to spend so much time together now that his dad was sober. The fact was, in his initial recovery, Mike's dad was so actively involved in AA, he spent less time at home than he had while he was drinking. Mike did not understand; he was confused and very angry, and he immediately reverted to his denial system in order to protect himself from the feelings he was experiencing.

It is essential for all family members to be familiar with the alcoholic's recovery program. When alcoholics regain sobriety, it is most helpful for them to have the support of other recovering people. A recovery program usually involves meetings, whether they are AA meetings, treatment program aftercare meetings, or other supportive groups. Most recovering people need to attend these meetings quite frequently, particularly when they first get sober. In Mike's case, his father probably really did need all those meetings. It is not sufficient for a counselor to explain this need to children and spouses. Mike needed his father to share feelings about the meetings, and to share his thoughts about sobriety. If parents find they need time away from families to attend meetings, it is important for them to explain and share with the family how vital and necessary this part of their recovery program is for them.

While the immediate and extended family can help children within the home understand alcoholism, not deny, and develop balanced coping mechanisms, it is advisable to also have the assistance of outside resources. Wherever help is sought, be aware that involving children often meets with their resistance. Many times, children believe they are handling their lives just fine, and it is the alcoholic who needs help, not them. Often, there is even more resistance if the alcoholic has been sober for a period of time, or is an absentee parent. Simply telling children you want them to be involved in therapy because they have been affected by the alcoholism in the family is not the most effective approach. Resistance stems from fear, anger, issues of trust and a sense of betrayal. Tell children it's necessary for them to attend because the drinking has caused a lot of turmoil in the family, and you want them to have the opportunity to address the problems the turmoil has created. Keep your explanations simple and don't enter into an argument over this issue. Explain that, while this is a family problem, they deserve special attention. Convey the attitude that they are worthy of this opportunity to learn how to handle problem situations. There is usually more resistance from teenagers than from preteens, but recognize all ages need this direction from you. Be firm. Request them to try therapy (counseling) for a specified number of times, say six. After that, together, you will decide if the program should be continued. Do recognize you can't make them participate in therapy forever, but if you can involve them initially, the resource itself often provides the sanctuary which will help them decide, on their own, to continue their involvement.

CHAPTER 6

The Adult Child

CHAPTER SIX

Upon reaching adulthood, the majority of children of alcoholics continue to experience problems related to trust, dependency, control, identification and expression of feelings. Adult children of alcoholics are a special population with special needs. Their belief that, "It will never happen to me" persists from early childhood into adulthood. This chapter speaks to these children as well as to those who work with adult children, about addressing such problematic issues.

If you are an adult child, this chapter is meant to help you identify and better understand some of your behavior patterns. It offers suggestions and courses of action which will enable you to initiate positive changes in your life.

Adult children of alcoholics have many identities. First and foremost, they are just that. . .adult children of alcoholics. Second, they may be the spouse or former spouse of an alcoholic. Third, they may be alcoholic themselves. Fourth, they could be any combination of the three.

If one is the spouse of an alcoholic, the issues of being the adult child, as well as being married to an alcoholic can be addressed simultaneously. Should drinking be a problem in the life of an adult child, the drinking itself must be examined and dealt with before other problems can be addressed. Adult children often question their own drinking, and rightly so, because of their higher than average tendency to become alcoholic. Appendix B is a self-exam which may indicate that the adult child seek counseling regarding his or her drinking behavior. If drinking is causing problems for adult children -- if they lack the ability to predict behavior when drinking, or lose the ability to control the frequency or quantity of what they drink -- these reasons are serious enough for them to seek counsel with an appropriate resource, an alcoholism professional. Until they achieve ongoing sobriety it is unlikely that these adult chidlren of alcoholics will be able to address the problems and issues created by their early environment. If adult children find drinking becomes an increasingly greater part of their lives, but truly believe drinking is not a problem, those adults should explore their reasons for increased drinking, and be very aware of their tendencies toward alcoholism.

When questioning your own drinking behavior, you, the adult child, do not have to know for certain whether or not you really are "alcoholic" before you reach out for help. The same holds true for other family members. All you need to know is that you're experiencing problems related to drinking.

I strongly suggest all children of alcoholics seek out assistance to help effect changes in their lives if they wish to develop a more satisfying life. Al-Anon is a viable resource which assists people to focus on themselves as well as to understand the issues of co-alcoholism. More recently, a specialized group of Al-Anon has been developed specifically for the adult child. While Al-Anon is a valuable resource, especially for children of alcoholics, professional therapists are also beginning groups for the adult child. There is much value in allowing oneself to be part of a group process. The identification with other adult children will provide immediate validation and support. Should specialized resources not be available, I suggest other helping professionals be sought out, i.e., marriage and family counselors, psychologists, social workers, etc. It might be helpful to offer this book as a reference. Tell them the issues mentioned herein are the areas you need to address. So many adult children have written or called me after reading or hearing of my work, saying, "I've been in therapy for years and I'm the child of an alcoholic. Until I read about your work and heard what you had to say, I never really understood." Some have said they have learned more about themselves by hearing about adult children than they had in 5, or even 10 years of therapy. So, it is important not just to seek therapy in general, but also to locate a resource person knowledgeable about the family dynamics of alcoholism.

Whether working individually with a therapist or in a group

process, it is important for you to make those close to you aware of your decision to seek counseling regarding the problems which have developed. It is important for those in your support system to be aware of your present vulnerability. Be it a lover, husband, wife, extended family, or friend, you will now need this support system more than ever to provide a strong backboard. This support should not be derived from young children within the home, but rather from peers. For this reason also, it is helpful to have other adult children of alcoholics with whom to identify and to lend mutual support.

In the earlier part of this book, I discussed, at length, why adult children have neither been able to trust, nor been able to talk. The single greatest problem area I have identified for adult children is their inability to ask others for what they need or for help. As you grow into adulthood, this inability to ask for help becomes an ongoing problem. You must begin to reach out and ask others to be available to you. You need to ask yourself:

When have I let another person be there for me?

When have I asked another person for help?

If only negative experiences are remembered, and it seems too difficult to take further risks, I would recommend therapy with a professional counselor.

As an exercise see if you can identify four people who are a part of your life, who would be available to you if you needed them. List the probable "helpers" for the little things, i.e. a neighbor to help you when your car won't start in the morning, a friend at work to take you to the airport, a personal friend to water your plants when you need to leave for the weekend. Identify those people who can help you in the areas where you feel most vulnerable, i.e., a specific friend to discuss concerns about problems at work, an intimate friend to share your fears related to making personal changes, a therapist to discuss your angers. The more important the situation is for you, the greater your need to feel safe will be. It is important for you to be willing to ask for help--even if you think you don't need it.

Before you, the adult child, are ready to continue in a therapeutic process, recognize two basic rights: 1) You have the right to talk about the real issues, and 2) you have the right to feel. You no longer have to pretend things are different from how they are, or were. There are legitimate reasons for the way you feel. There are reasons for the craziness and the confusion you experience. By focusing on these issues, you are not blaming anyone for the situation but simply trying to readjust and live in a way which allows openness, honesty and love to be a normal, healthy part of your life.

Many adult children think if they are angry that they must scream or if they are unhappy they must leave the situation. Adult children have a high tendency to make absolute decisions related to the experience of a particular feeling, such as changing jobs, moving or leaving a spouse. These reactions are not necessary. Acceptance of feelings, i.e. anger or joy, without a harsh judgment and a related major decision, combined with the ability to express feeings will decrease fear and feelings of alienation toward oneself. Feelings seem inappropriate only when they are not understood.

Adult children are generally fearful of feelings because they don't understand them. Feelings aren't understood because adult children have not had the guidance to put them into perspective. Years ago, as small children they began rolling their feelings up in a bundle like a small piece of snow rolling down a hill and these feelings have now become a giant snowball. By the time the snowball reaches the bottom of the hill--by the time the children have grown up--the feelings have simply been stored up, bad feelings upon bad feelings. No wonder adult children are scared. Now, when they do get in touch with all their feelings, down to the very core, they are overwhelmed. This is why it is valuable to be involved with others in a therapeutic setting. The therapeutic process can provide the safety and protection adult children need as they become more aware of their feelings. The balance of this chapter will offer insight and lead to greater understanding and resolution of major problem areas for the adult child.

FEELINGS

The following is an exercise related to feelings in general. It is meant to be of assistance in helping the adult child who has difficulty identifying or expressing feelings.

Fill in the boxes of the feelings you identify with. Do you ever feel?

love	☐	ashamed	☐
fear	☐	happy	☐
warmth	☐	shy	☐
worry	☐	excited	☐
caring	☐	guilty	☐
sadness	☐	sympathy	☐
patient	☐	moody	☐
confused	☐	discouraged	☐
violent	☐	frustration	☐
angry	☐	brave	☐
hurt	☐	sensitive	☐
embarrassed	☐	humorous	☐
jealous	☐	gloomy	☐
understanding	☐	encouraged	☐
hatred	☐		

Identify verbally or better yet, list in written form when and where you experience those feelings. If the identification of feelings is difficult, make copies of this page and on a daily or weekly basis acknowledge to yourself what feelings you have been experiencing. Try to share these with another person. The more specific you can be about your feelings, the more you can understand and accept them, and the more apt you are to be able to do something constructive about them. While positive feelings are the ones people seek, negative feelings can be viewed as cues or signals that can give one information about what is needed. "When I feel sad, it may possibly mean I need support." "When I am angry, I probably need to clarify my stance." "When I am scared I need to let someone else know that."

By viewing the more painful feelings as signals it is easier to accept them and to utilize them constructively. By identifying feelings one is less apt to be overwhelmed by emotion and end up depressed, confused or enraged.

* * * * * *

With this exercise you can gain insight and awareness to family patterns. This will assist the adult child in understanding how the expression of feelings is often learned behavior from parental role modeling.

On a scale of 1-5, one being the least often expressed, 5 being the most often expressed, rate your parents frequency of expression.

MOTHER	FATHER	FEELINGS	MOTHER	FATHER	FEELINGS
12345	12345	love	12345	12345	shame
12345	12345	fear	12345	12345	happiness
12345	12345	warmth	12345	12345	shyness
12345	12345	worry	12345	12345	excitement
12345	12345	caring	12345	12345	guilt
12345	12345	sadness	12345	12345	sympathy
12345	12345	patience	12345	12345	moodiness
12345	12345	confusion	12345	12345	discouragement
12345	12345	violence	12345	12345	frustration
12345	12345	anger	12345	12345	bravery
12345	12345	hurt	12345	12345	sensitivity
12345	12345	embarassment	12345	12345	humor
12345	12345	jealousy	12345	12345	gloom
12345	12345	understanding	12345	12345	encouragement
12345	12345	hate			

You can also ask yourself which feelings did you want expressed more, and which ones less? Can you see any repetitive patterns for you in adulthood?

Crying

Young children of alcoholics generally have learned not to cry, or to cry silently alone and adult children often continue in the same pattern. Thirty-six year old adult child, Jerry, now a recovering alcoholic, was talking about the issue of crying. He told of how he was the child who never cried. When he was very young, he remembered crying only once, and that was when a pet died. He entered into adolescence and adulthood being "tough" and "surviving". Jerry told his counselor about his complete inability to shed tears over any of his personal misfortunes which included nine hospitalizations for alcoholism. Surrender is essential for an alcoholic's recovery. It includes the breaking of the denial system about one's situation in life, mentally, emotionally, physically and spiritually. Jerry's surrender began when the tears started to flow the day he was admitted to his tenth alcoholic hospital program. Jerry needed to cry--he needed to quit being "tough", "alone", and in the denial trap of not talking, not feeling and not trusting. The tears were the break-through. If you are an adult child who can identify with patterns of not crying, or crying alone and silently, you must understand the necessity of breaking the pattern before you will be able to effect your own recovery process. This surrender is the first step in recovery whether or not you are alcoholic.

While many adult children follow the forementioned pattern, there are those adult children who find themselves crying, yet not understanding the reason for the tears. Some may, periodically, lose the ability to control their crying. Some find they are crying at inappropriate times, while others find they cry at the appropriate times, but there is an over-abundance of tears. Cheryl, 35, says, "I'm so tired of crying, I never cried as a child, and today I cry at the least little thing. I cry if I get scared, I cry if I feel rejected, I cry if I hear a sad story on the news, I cry when I read a nice, warm story in the paper. I don't seem to have any control. It's really embarassing, but more than anything, it really scares me."

It is important for you, the adult child, to 1) recognize the need to cry, 2) give yourself permission to cry, 3) let another person know about this, and 4) let that other person be available to be supportive of you. You will need to re-evaluate the messages you previously received about crying, such as, "It doesn't do any good to cry." "Boys don't cry." "Only sissies cry." "I'll smack you harder if you cry." New messages need to be, "It's okay if I cry." "It's important that I allow myself to cry." "It's a healthy release." "I'll probably feel better."

All adult children need to address the issues of crying.

Ask yourself:

When do you cry?

Do you ever cry?

Do you only cry when alone?

Do you cry hard or do you cry slowly and silently?

Do you cry because people hurt your feelings?

Do you cry for no apparent reason?

Do others know when you cry?

Do others see you cry?

Do others hear you cry?

Do you let others comfort you when you cry?

Do you let others hold you?

Do you let them just sit with you?

What do you do to prevent yourself from crying?

Do you tell yourself you are stupid for letting another person hurt your feelings?

Do you get angry with yourself for crying?

How is your pattern as an adult different from that of a child?

What did you do with your tears as a child?

Did you cry?

Did others know when you were crying?

Did you let others comfort you when you were crying?

What did you do then to prevent yourself from crying?

Read through these questions again, slowly, then share what you know about yourself with another person. Pick a person with whom you feel safe, a therapist, an Al-Anon member, a friend; someone with whom you feel you can allow yourself to be vulnerable. Remember, others may have old messages about the stigma of crying too, and might welcome the opportunity to talk about an issue many people never take the time to explore.

You may also need to think about the basis of your fear of crying. For the super-controlling person, fear of crying usually means a fear of falling apart. It is a fear of losing control; the fear that once crying starts, it will lead to hysterical behavior or that you will be unable to stop. The greater your fear, the greater the need to let others offer support. Recognize the need to establish a situation which is both protective and healthy. Now, recognize when you cry, which you will need to do--that cry is exactly what you will do. You may cry for five minutes, even ten minutes. While crying may feel very frightening, you do not need to go into hysteria, nor will you. As a therapist, I have seen hundreds of people cry, and they never needed to be carted away! With the help of your group and/or therapist, you will be able to sort out the reasons for crying. Remember, you have accumulated a great deal of unresolved feelings. . .your tears are usually related to sorrow, confusion, lonliness and loss.

Fear

As adults, children of alcoholics often experience an overwhelming sense of fear. Much of the time that fear is unidentifiable. These fearful times are often episodic, in that extreme high and low mood swings are experienced. The adult child may also experience periods of extreme fearfulness contrasted by periods totally devoid of fear. On the other hand they may find themselves existing in a perpetual state of unidentifiable fear.

Many adult children are fearful of expressing their needs, fearing a loss of love should they express a want. Dawn, an adult child said, "I've grown a lot, but I still feel gut level fear when I express my wants and needs to my husband. It's difficult to be spontaneously open and self-disclosing. I'm afraid he won't love me." As these children of alcoholics become adults many of them continue to experience fear of confrontation. For so many adult children, confrontation is simple disagreement, or questioning--but the fear is, nonetheless, intense and based on what they perceived to be a real confrontation. These fears may stem from years of harassment by a parent, which always resulted in the child feeling guilty or humiliated. These fears persist, also, because there was never any normal disagreement in their alcoholic homes. Any expressed disagreement resulted in yelling and loud arguing because the alcoholic could not tolerate anyone disagreeing with him/her. Disagreement was perceived by the alcoholic as betrayal, and resulted in actions which belittled and condemned the child. Adult children who experienced a lot of fear of the unknown as children, never knowing what to expect next, would continue to experience uncertainty and fear of the unknown as an adult. The fear of the unknown can keep one immobilized, and being stuck in fear, itself, immobilizes one emotionally. It will result in a tendency for people to discount their own perceptions and not have the courage to check out other people's perceptions. The results are isolation, depression and low self-esteem.

When I think about my dad drinking again I get shakey inside.

I feel scared about things and worry alot when everything is ok. I feel tied up and can't let go. I want to untie the knots and be free.

Janice, 44

Take the time to read and respond to the following questions:
What did you fear as a child?
Did you fear you were going to be left alone?
Were you afraid you were going to get hit?
Were you afraid your mom or your dad did not love you?

What did you do when you were fearful as a child?
Did you go to your room and cry?
Did you get angry instead?
Did you hide in a closet?
Did you ask a brother or sister to come and be with you?
Did others know that you were afraid?
Do you think your mom knew?
Do you think your sister, or your grandparents possibly knew?
How did you express this fear?
Did you wet the bed?
Did you mask your fear with anger?
How is that pattern similar in your adulthood?
Do you still go off by yourself when afraid?
Do you still get angry instead?
Are you sharing your fears with someone, or are you still
     pretending you're not afraid?

Ask those questions of another adult, and share your answers
with one another. Share with someone you trust.

Anger

Anger is a feeling which has seldom been acknowledged by
the adult child. It is important for you to find a supportive environment, become more aware of your anger and then express it.
First, consider the possibility that you have unresolved anger. Second, remember, it is a normal human emotion to be angry.

The feeling of anger is natural to everyone, but for the child of the
alcoholic, it is a feeling which is often repressed, twisted and
distorted. It is feeling which is invariably denied, yet manifests
itself in a multitude of ways--depressive behavior, overeating,
oversleeping, placating and psychosomatic problems. A woman
told me about her fear of anger. She said she feared other
people's anger because she herself never felt anger. She was
unaware she even had any anger of her own. Children from
alcoholic homes rarely experience healthy role modeling for the
expression of their anger. In the alcoholic home anger is often
expressed through a tense silence, through mutual blaming, or
one-sided blaming coupled with one-sided acceptance. These

family members find that any expression of anger seldom solves problems, showing anger only creates more problems. Should violence be a threat, or an actuality, an even greater than average fear of another person's anger would be present.

Another woman, an adult child of an alcoholic, told me, after four years of a marriage in which there were very few arguments, she woke her husband one morning and said, "I'm leaving now, " and smiled. She said there had been no discussion of her wanting out of the marriage, nor her wanting anything to be different. She said she wasn't angry, she simply wanted out. She explained she had never been allowed to argue about anything as a child, and when her husband raised his voice, she'd simply agree to his wants. She walked out of a marriage which possibly could have been saved had she had the ability simply to disagree; had she had the ability to express what it was she needed or wanted. But for her, the fear of dealing with anger, either her own or her husband's, was too great to risk.

Other adult children identify more with Lee, age 31, who was aware of his anger, but didn't find outlets for expression. "I have needed to let go of the bitterness and hatred. I see I have denied myself so much, like relaxing, being held, just being."

Lee acknowledged that, with the help of a few good friends and through the love of God, he worked through his problems that stemmed from his painful past. He ended his letter to me saying, "I have learned to let go of the pain and be free." While some adult children have repressed their anger, and others have twisted it into hate or bitterness--all have a definite need to resolve issues which arose as a result of their anger.

The following exercise will help the very understanding, forever nice adult child to identify anger and express it, and will help those already capable of identifying anger to separate the issues and be less overwhelmed by their feelings. Hopefully, you will also realize what one does with anger is learned and can be reshaped to better meet your own needs. Remember, feelings are a natural part of you, use them as signals to help direct you.

Make a list of all the things you could have been angry about as a child.

Example: I could have been angry at my dad for hitting my mom when she was drunk.

I could have been angry at my dad for giving my dog away.

I could have been angry the time my mom passed out on Christmas Eve.

I could have been angry at my mom for not listening to me when I told her dad was drunk.

1. _____

2. _____

3. _____

4. _____

Now, make a list of things which, as an adult, you could be angry about, but aren't

Example: I could be angry with my dad for never getting sober.

I could be angry with my sister for never going to see my mom.

I could be angry with my husband for not being more willing to listen to me when I want to talk about my mom or dad.

I could be angry when I think people have taken advantage of me.

1. _____

2. _____

3. _____

4. _____

When you have approximately four or five examples of situations in which you could be angry as a child or adult, draw a large "X" across the words "I could be" in every one of those sentences. Then write, "I am," "I was" or "I am still," depending on whether or not you are still angry.

Example: I am still angry at my dad for hitting my mom.
I am angry with my dad for never getting sober.
I am still angry with my dad for giving my dog away.
I was angry the time my mom passed out on Christmas Eve.
I am angry when people take advantage of me.
I am still angry at my mom for not listening to me when I told her dad was drunk.
I am angry with my husband for not being more willing to listen to me when I talk about my mom or dad.

Now, reflect on those sentences and thought--be aware of how you feel.

Do you feel angry?
Do you feel numb?
Does this cause you to have a headache?

After answering these questions admit to yourself how you feel right now.

If you are working on this exercise with someone, tell them how you feel. Is it difficult to admit your feelings? Some of you will find relief in simply acknowledging your past pain. Others won't like the feelings at all. Remember, acknowledging anger, as well as other feelings, is a necessary part of the recovery, and the more you share your experiences with yourself and with others, the easier recovery will be for you. A secondary benefit is an increased closeness and bond with those friends with whom you choose to share your feelings.

Ask yourself now:

What did you do with your anger as a child?
Did you swallow and not become aware of it?
Did you play the piano extra hard?
Did you hit your brothers and sisters?
Did you go to your room and cry?
What did your other family members do with their anger?
Did your dad just drink more?
Did your mom just drink more?
Did your one brother just shrug his shoulders and go outside and play with his friends?
Did your sister just sort of cry silently?
Are you afraid you will go into a rage?
Are you afraid you will start crying to the point of becoming hysterical?
is there a fear about what would happen if you really acknowledged your anger today?

Talk with others about their anger. Ask them what they get angry about. Ask them how they express their anger. Compare patterns. You'll find out you are not alone.

Guilt

Imagine holding on to guilt for 10, 30, possibly as many as 60 years. . .especially guilt about something over which one has absolutely no control. When children are constantly made to feel guilty, they invariably continue adding more and more guilt to their inner selves as they grow up.

Whenever I think of the guilt children of alcoholics feel, I am reminded of a special child of an alcoholic father I once met. He came to me asking if I would participate in a task force for a local helping agency. After he had introduced himself and told me about the needs of the agency, he admitted he was not familiar with my work, but had been told by others that I worked with "kids whose parents are alcoholic."

I acknowledged the information he had been given was correct, and I began explaining the nature of what I do. I had only been speaking for about 3-4 minutes when he interrupted me suddenly, saying, "Yeah,. . .yeah. . .my dad was alcoholic. Uh, he died." His gaze dropped from my eyes, and he began looking fixedly at the floor. "Yeah," he said "I was 13." His gaze turned to the ceiling. "He was 31 or 32, I guess. Died in an accident. He was drunk when it happened." Haltingly, he continued, "You know, I never understood. I never understood. You know I tried to be good. I never knew what he wanted though. I know I did things he didn't like, but I wasn't a bad kid. . ."

Mr. Jacobsen was 74-years old when he confessed his feelings of guilt to me. He was not rambling in semi-senility but feeling pure guilt. He still believed he was responsible, somehow, for his father's drinking and ultimately, his father's death. This adult child carried more than 61 years of guilt because he had no understanding of the alcoholic disease process.

Another adult man told me, "I have carried guilt feelings throughout my life because I didn't want the responsibility of raising my brother and sisters. I deserted my mom when I was 18 and joined the Army. I deserted her -- just like my alcoholic father." A woman adult child once pointed out she had been seriously working on issues around guilt for 1-½ years in Al-Anon "I have a lot of issues to deal with about my mother, her constant criticism, guilt because I didn't know why I was being criticized, and finally, my guilt for being alive."

Children of alcoholics need to reassess those things for which they held themselves responsible. The Serenity Prayer, which is the hallmark of AA and Al-Anon philosophies says, "God, grant me the serenity to accept the things I cannot change, the courage to change the things I can, and the wisdom to know the difference." The more you understand, the easier it is to accept that you aren't responsible for your parent's alcoholism. As an adult, it is important that you realize that as a young child you had only emotional, psychological and physical capabilities to behave as just that -- a child. When you have accepted that, it is easier not to be so self-blaming and guilt-ridden.

Think about what guilts you still carry. Do you every say, "If only I had. . .?" Take some time right now to examine your guilt feelings by working the following exercise.

As a child, if only I had:

1. _____

2. _____

3. _____

As a teenager, if only I had:

1. _____

2. _____

3. _____

Now, seriously answer, would any other 6-year old, 12-year-old, or 18-year-old in the same situation with the same circumstances, have behaved any differently? In fact, even as a 25-year-old, or a 35-year-old, without a knowledge of alcoholism and its many ramifications would it be possible to respond differently? As an adult, the tendency to accept all guilt is a pattern which needs to be broken.

Now, ask yourself:
What did I do with my guilt as a child?
Was I forever apologizing?
Was I a perfect child making up for what I thought I was doing wrong?
Was I an angry child?

Adult children have spent many years integrating guilt into a part of their basic psychological makeup. Consequently, it will take time to release that guilt, but it is not impossible. Theodore Isaac Rubin's book called, 'The Angry Book," discusses ways people twist their anger so it becomes unrecognizable as anger.

This disguise is usable for all feelings, including guilt. Many times, when people feel guilty, they end up crying, looking as if they were sad or disappointed, or twisting the guilt into anger. Disguising one's true feelings by putting up a false front is common practice. Out of the need to survive, people will create distorted expressions of feelings. What do you feel guilty about? The little things in everyday life? Everything in everyday life? What do you do when you feel guilt? Do you buy presents for the person you feel guilty in reference to? Do you get depressed? Do you get angry? Do you berate yourself?

A simple exercise when you are feeling guilty, is to ask yourself, "What did I do to affect the situation? What can I do to make it any different? Can I accept that I did all that I was able to do with the resources available?" Give yourself permission to make mistakes. Take responsibility for what is yours, but don't accept responsibility for what is not yours. You will need to work on your self-image and your ability to understand and express your own fear and anger, as well as to learn ways to deal with your guilt.

* * * * * *

The possibilities for masking feelings are many. Anxiety, depression, overeating, insomnia, over-sleeping, high blood pressure, overwork, always being sick, always being tired, being overly nice -- the list goes on. These consequences not only affect your life, but they will interfere with your relationships with others, your spouse, your lover, your children, your friends. Now is the time to change the pattern, but please don't try to do it in a vacuum. Let others be a part of this new growth.

Daughters of The Bottle

until i was twenty-two
i didn't think anyone else
had a drunk for a mother
then i met   lori   joannie   and   susan
i recognized them immediately
by their stay away smiles
they were leaders in their work
competent imposters
like me
who would say they were sorry
if somebody bumped into them
on a crowded street
i call on them
once in a while
they always come
children of alcoholics
always do

Jane, adult child

* * * * * *

RESHAPING ROLES -- AS AN ADULT CHILD

Responsible

For that extremely responsible person, the person who has the ability to accomplish a great deal, the issue of control often creates problem areas in adult life. Accompanying a strong need to be in control is an extreme fear of being totally out of control, particularly with feelings. As one woman told me, "If I permitted myself to throw one plate out of frustration, there would be nothing stopping me from throwing 30!"

As mentioned earlier, extremely responsible, overachieving young people often become very rigid and controlling adults. They find it is necessary for them to manipulate other people. If you are a controlling person, it is essential for you to examine your need to be in control. For one thing, controlling provides security, and not being in control would mean total insecurity. If you were to relinquish areas of control in your life today, you would probably feel you were losing total control but, in fact, your environment would not fall apart around you. Controlling persons never allow themselves to test the experience of giving up control. As an exercise, think about what areas of control you might be willing to give up. Over a given time period, try to relinquish control in some of those areas. If you are willing to try this exercise, begin by giving up control in those areas which seem least threatening to you. Retain control in those areas which are most threatening for you.

Think about what might happen if you gave up certain areas of control. What if you let others make decisions about things in your life? What if you gave up taking charge in certain areas of your home and work life. Think about what might happen if you were not involved in special decisions or projects. In all probability, someone else would step in and take charge. In all likelihood, the result may not be the same as yours would have been. It's possible the situation may not be handled as well as you would have handled it, but heaven forbid, it may be handled even better than had you been in charge!

Remember, as you give up control, you may feel some insecurity, but amazingly, you will have more energy and more time to relax. You won't feel as rigid and structured because you will not be expending all your energy trying to keep everything and everybody in order. It's important you fill the empty time with something which allows you to feel more comfortable with yourself.

A lot of awkwardness will result as you try to address the issue of letting go of control of your life, your job, your family. It is often a real breakthrough for you, the responsible adult child, to recognize the imbalance in your life. Many times, this very recognition is sufficient impetus for you to begin reprioritizing your time and behavior. Some may discover a need to talk with others and get help in order to structure your "play time," which is a necessary part of a balanced life. "To play? To relax? I know I need to. It's just so hard to find the time." says 30-year-old Janice. Howard, age 32, says, "I took two weeks vacation, because of stress-related physical problems. All I did was work. I just never could find the time to just relax!" Overcontrolling and overworking adult children need to think about, and talk about, the issues of play and fun. Many adult children of alcoholics never found the time to play as children and now, as adults, they find they don't know how to play. They were very busy and serious as children. When they grow up they are simply very serious, busy adults.

Adult children often tell me of the awkwardness, or the embarrassment, they experience when trying to play. Many feel guilty for taking time out to relax. It is important to discuss these feelings when they are experienced. Adult responsible children of alcoholics need to know there is a part of them that is spontaneous and fun loving -- a part of them that has been buried since childhood -- a part that has been repressed for too long. They need to know that they can relax, laugh and feel good about themselves, and in so doing, they can still successfully relate to other people.

In the beginning, you may find yourself even structuring the play periods. Because your tendencies have been to structure everything in your life, now, as you are unlearning a part of that process, it is acceptable to use a certain amount of structure to play. (You may find commercial relaxation tapes/cassettes helpful.) On a daily basis, ask yourself what you could do just for yourself -- that is, give to yourself -- that doesn't involve control. Consider taking a walk, visiting an art gallery, or relaxing on the beach. Relaxing may mean just sitting under your favorite tree. Probably, the first few times you take a walk, you will think about all the things you are not getting done at home, or at work. Be aware that it takes time to become comfortable with this process. Change your relaxation patterns gradually, instead of buying magazines related to work, buy magazines which are light reading. Instead of watching others play a game, become involved in the game yourself. You may need to force these changes, and they may be awkward initially, however, in time, you will enjoy the new you.

Fun Game

Make a list of things you've always wanted to do, of fun activities you may or may not ever participate in. Go through those and ask yourself if any of these are possible, or if you could participate in any of these activities. Circle the ones which you could easily do. Then, double circle the ones you are willing to try in the next week. Now, start doing them!

1.

2.

3.

4.

5.

6.

7.

8.

9.

10.

11.

12.

13.

14.

15.

Another positive change for you is to risk asking other people to be available for you to offer support and guidance. At first, choose those people with whom you feel the safest. Should you decide not to choose your best friend, consider a therapist. Whoever you select, pick the people you think are the least risky in terms of being willing to respond to you. It is important for you to ask for their help -- even if you think you don't need it.

Controlling adult children certainly have to learn to deal with feelings. A part of the need to be in control stems from not wanting to feel and not wanting to experience the pain caused by feelings. Being in charge, or in control, has usually been the only way these people have developed an ability to feel good about themselves.

While high self-esteem is often based on the positives of this Responsible role, usually the controlling person will not feel such positive self-worth in other areas of life. As you reshape your life, you can retain pride in your ability to accomplish, but you also need to develop a greater sense of spontaneity, and a greater ability to interact with others in a less rigid manner. You will be able to give up some areas of control only after you learn to identify your feelings and to express these feelings in a manner which feels safe to you.

Adjuster

The children who were more detached, possibly more nondescript than the responsible, placating or acting-out children -- the adjusters, will need to take a look at how they feel about themselves. The adjusters have operated on the premise that "life is easier if you don't draw attention to yourself." They need to give themselves new messages which communicate that they are very important people and, sometimes, they deserve attention for themselves because they are very special. Adjusters have lots of feelings which they have not had the opportunity to examine, feelings which they have not had the opportunity to share with others.

Adjusting adults continue to survive usually living their lives in a very malleable fashion. They need to recognize that, at times, it is healthier and more satisfying not to be so flexible. Because adjusters make very few waves for other people, they have no sense of direction for themselves. They lack purpose or a feeling of fulfillment. It is like always being along just for the ride -- one feels a sense of movement, yet often, one only travels in circles.

One adult child revealed that her husband decided to move five times, taking her to five states in the first four years of their marriage. She said she didn't realize she could have discouraged any of the moves and in fact, could have refused to go. She said she always did what he wanted. In retrospect, her adjusting was not good for her husband, nor for their relationship.

If you are such an adjusting adult, you need daily practice in identifying the power you do have in your life. Here is a four part exercise that will help you do just that.

Part 1. At the beginning of each day, you need to write down at least five options you have that day.

For example:
1. I choose whether or not I eat breakfast.
2 . I choose where I buy gas for the car.
3 . I choose whom I sit with at lunch.
4 . I choose which television show I watch.
5 . I choose the time I go to bed.

Recognize that these five options are certainly not major decisions but in the beginning, it is wise to start with the small areas of daily life one can change. This exercise should be done consistently for a period of one week.

Part 2. Continue this exercise for a second week listing 10 choices which can be made on a daily basis. The goal of this exercise is to teach you to acknowledge your power in making choices. By the third or fourth day, you will begin to feel the power.

Part 3. After following through with the above exercise practice on a daily basis making notes of existing options which were not acted upon. List three per day. Continue this part of the exercise for one week.

For Example:

I chose not to assume my power by not responding when. . .

1. I went to lunch with friends at a Japanese restaurant and I hate Japanese food.
2. My daughter took the car for the evening when I wanted to use it.
3. I knew I was short-changed $1.60 at the grocery store, but didn't speak up.

The purpose of doing this is to help you to recognize your power to choose, even though that power is not always exercised. This will develop your sense of choice.

Part 4. After each day's documentation, make a log of what could have been done differently should the situation occur again. Even if you do not take that different action, list a few alternative responses. Should other alternatives not come to mind, another person, a friend, a therapist, someone that you respect may be able to recommend an option. Practice exercises 3 and 4 together for another week. They can both be repeated as often as you feel the need.

If you are an adjuster who is attempting to change watch for certain clues. Should you begin to experience boredom, depression, or a sense of helplessness, it is time to become reacquainted with power and options. Practice the aforementioned exercises again. Discuss this process with another, share the fun of having so many choices, and allow yourself to feel some pride in this new awareness.

Placater

For the adult children who spend so much time taking care of other people's needs, it is important for them to understand the word "selfish." They have perfected the inability to give to themselves nor can they consider their own needs. The placater's role is always to attend to the feelings and wants of another. As adult placaters proceed in recovery, it is natural for them to feel guilty for focusing on themselves.

When I decide to put myself first for a change, I feel very guilty and have trouble differentiating between putting myself first and being selfish.
                                        Kathleen, age 31

Remember, you are learning how to give to yourself, and that is not bad. In order to be willing to give to yourself, it is vital to look at old messages which may need to be changed.

New messages may be:
I don't <u>HAVE</u> to take care of everyone else.
I <u>HAVE</u> choices about how I respond to people.
My needs <u>ARE</u> important.
I have feelings, <u>I'M</u> scared, <u>I AM</u> angry!
It is <u>OKAY</u> to put my own well-being first.
Some situations can be resolved <u>WITHOUT</u> my being involved.
<u>OTHERS</u> can lend support to those who need it when I am not willing to be available.
I'm <u>NOT GUILTY</u> because others feel bad.

This should only be the beginning of a list of new messages. To the adult placating child, I suggest you find the messages which fit your situation and make a list of them. On a daily basis, for a minimum of a month, read and reread these messages aloud to yourself.

You will feel some of the old guilt for awhile, but it will be mixed with a new sensation -- that of excitement along with a sense of aliveness. I believe in people giving themselves credit and being their own best friends, so do not be embarrassed about stroking yourself and being important to yourself.

Fifty-four-year-old Maureen said she spent her life trying to be everybody's "good little girl." She walked a very narrow line, afraid to do anything which might cause anyone's disapproval. "Slowly, I have learned it is much more important for me to consider my own needs and feelings, and how important it is for me to act on them." This is the type of freedom all adult children can attain. Maureen knows the process is slow. It is not easy to give up fears and try new behaviors. But, it is possible!

If you are an adult child and think you fit into the placater's role, examine how you give. On a daily basis, document all the little things you do for people. Itemize each one. After you have read your list of anywhere from 50 to 100 items, are you tired? Of course you are tired. Where will you find the energy to give to yourself? The answer -- you won't. Ask yourself if each of these placating acts was absolutely necessary. Could you have backed off a little? As you attempt to back off on giving, you need to start work on being able to receive. All true placaters need to work on receiving.

Ask yourself about your capacity to receive. Do you "yes, but. . ." when you are complimented? Do you change the subject when you are commended? Are you embarrassed, or do you feel awkward when you receive a gift? Can you enjoy the moment? You may need to give yourself new messages regarding receiving:

I <u>DESERVE</u> to be given a thank you.
I can <u>ENJOY</u> being the recipient of praise.
I will take time to <u>HEAR</u> my praise, <u>SMILE</u> and soak it in.

For a minimum of two weeks, pay strict attention to receiving. Practice your new messages.

Many people attempting to make changes sometimes fear they will go to the other extreme. Remember, it is okay to enjoy yourself. Don't worry about becoming totally egocentric. If you have spent years people-pleasing, you will never totally lose that tendency, besides when you give up some giving, you will have more energy to receive. While it may be awkward at first, in time you will experience pure enjoyment. Whichever pattern is yours, keep receiving.

As you change role patterns by being more spontaneous and more willing to follow (the responsible one), by making more decisions and being more assertive (adjuster), and giving more to yourself (placater), others will be responding to the new you in a variety of ways. Remember, they also have choices about how they respond. Many will welcome the change and adjust accordingly in the relationship. Those who want to manipulate you in order to have their needs met, may attempt to sabotage your efforts. Recognize that they also have some fear about the change, about how you relate to them. However others respond, you will like yourself better as you develop the ability to give to yourself a part of your wholeness which has been denied for too long. Keep in mind that you deserve your gift to yourself.

CHAPTER 7

Family Violence

Physical Abuse
Sexual Abuse

In retrospect, most adult children who were raised in alcoholic homes remember the frequent arguing which took place in the home. Some remember that the arguing centered around "money" or "the kids," most say the arguing was about "anything and everything." Both the children and the nonalcoholic parent experience a significant amount of verbal harassment, no matter whether they are right or wrong. The impressions and feelings caused by this harassment remain with those children, and are carried into adulthood. In some instances, the harassment can escalate and suddenly erupt into violence, and result in physical or sexual assault. While the direct correlation between alcoholism and physical and/or sexual abuse has not been clearly delineated, a strong association between these problems is consistently identified. For these reasons, it is necessary to address the issues of spouse and child battering and incest.

The following sections are designed to give a brief overview of the interrelatedness between alcoholism and physical and/or sexual abuse. These sections will exlain why, when both problems exist in a family, both must be identified and treated.

PHYSICAL ABUSE

While dad's drinking increased, mom became more erratic. She was playful and fun one moment, and full of rage the next. She would pick up anything (whip, vacuum cleaner hose, spoon) and hit and hit and hit, and would never apologize. Even when we were bleeding, somehow it was still our fault.

Cindy, age 34

Alcoholism and domestic violence alike are dangerous and potentially fatal problems not only for the victims but for other family members as well. Social service professionals frequently discover these two problems occurring simultaneously in many families. Yet, while either the alcoholism or the violence may be addressed as a separate issue, it is very seldom that both problems are addressed and treated simultaneously. The National Council on Alcoholism estimates as many as 60 percent of the alcoholic families now in treatment have experienced domestic violence. My own research indicates 66 percent of children raised in alcoholic families have been physically abused, or have witnessed abuse of another family member. In more than one-third of these families, such abuse occurs on a regular basis.

The nonalcoholic spouse, a child (or children) may be abused. It is important to recognize, however, that the violent person is not always the alcoholic, as Cindy's experience confirms. The alcoholic also can be the victim of violence. Thus, either the alcoholic or the nonalcoholic spouse may be the batterer; the alcoholic, the nonalcoholic spouse and/or the children may all be victims. To make matters worse, some children may live in a home where both parents are alcoholic and both parents are batterers.

When we think of physical abuse, a picture of a badly beaten, chronically black and blue child comes to mind. In reality, battering may be much more subtle and infrequent, with barely visible results. Battering can occur in the form of pushing and shoving, grabbing, pinching, or choking. Abuse can be mental as well as verbal and physical. In many alcoholic homes, only terror exists; no bruises attesting to violence are evident. Children and spouses frequently experience intensely frightening and physically dangerous situations. When dad, in an alcoholic siege, takes the family for a 60 mph auto ride down a mountain road at night with the headlights turned off, the effect is just as traumatic as any physical violence, yet leaves no physical scars. Emotional violence, however, frequently carries the potential for physical violence. Family members often resist identifying battering until it reaches the stage of bruises or broken bones, and until it has increased in frequency and it occurs on nearly a daily basis.

While alcoholism and battering are not always related, it is helpful to examine similarities in the dynamics of both, when experienced in the home. Both the batterer and the alcoholic minimize and deny their abusive behaviors. They will discount their acts and minimize the severity of their drunkenness or battering. Both have strong tendencies to blame others, neither will accept the responsibility for their own behavior and both exhibit Jeckyll and Hyde personality changes. Children may experience an overly nice, caring parent who, after taking a few drinks, becomes a raging lion. In this case the batterer, simply erupts like a volcano for what appears to be no apparent reason. Both the alcoholic and batterer learn to rationalize their behavior, and invariably, there is (in their own rationale) a good reason (excuse) for the drinking or for the violent behavior. Episodic violence and drinking occur more and more frequently as these unhealthy lifestyles progress. Inevitably, for the alcoholic and the batterer, the drinking and the violence begin to cause more trauma and more problems in almost all areas of family and personal life. The alcoholic and the batterer increasingly feel more guilty and more remorseful. They frequently attempt to regain control, they make promises and create false hopes. The cycle continues indefinitely, unless the alcoholic and batterer are treated.

Both spouses and children of alcoholics and batterers tend to minimize the impact of the drinking and violence on the family. This is the family's denial process. Family members accept the blame because they believe that had they been better in their roles, (a better wife, or a better child) the batterer/alcoholic would have no reason to get so upset, fly into rages and drink. The denial processes of NOT FEELING, NOT TRUSTING AND NOT TALKING permeate the family. Alcoholism, when coupled with violence, doubles the need for denial and creates an even greater sense of helplessness in the lives of family members. When children don't show obvious signs of being emotionally effected by violence, it is important to recognize that it is probably due to denial. Children in battered families will develop an almost identical denial process as the children in alcoholic homes and in both situations, they practice denial to a greater extent. Role patterns in the violent home are often similar to those seen in alcoholic homes, only with an even greater intensity due to the dual problem. Remember, the goal of family members in attempting to live through these problems is the same -- minimize the conflict, adjust, placate, act-out, drop out - do anything, but be sure to survive.

Consequences for Children

Research relating to domestic violence shows that witnessing violence may be just as detrimental to the emotional and psychological development of a child, as if the child were actually being abused. Just as children who are abused tend to be abusers themselves in adulthood, children who witness assault on parents or siblings, also tend to be abusers and/or abused victims in adulthood. Many children of alcoholics become alcoholic and/or marry alcoholics; many children of batterers become batterers and/or marry batterers; many children of both, do both.

When dad drank, someone got beat. We hated to see him get started, but the quarreling was awful loud. My mom was hurt a lot. How did he get started on me? Simple. I defended my mom and if he wanted to know who did something, rather than see my younger brother or sisters get it, I did it! No matter what it was. He usually used a wooden hanger or marine belt on us. I still look

*out for my brother and sisters and my mom; I
wouldn't lift a finger to help my dad. I refused to
go to his funeral or send flowers. I am the same
with my own kids, take care of them, protect them
from my ex-husband, who somehow has managed
to develop a dependency on prescription drugs,
always has a beer in his hand, and likes to hit.*
Sharon, Age 37

Treatment

For those of you who are victims of violence, or parents of victims, your foremost concern should be to seek and/or provide protection for yourself and for your family. In every state, services are available to help both adult and child victims. Crisis hotlines exist in most communities and can refer you to proper resources. Victims may need to call the local rape or battering hotline, or contact a shelter to learn about specific resources for women.

If an appropriate hotline is not available to you, the police often have their own hotline which addresses such problems. Hospital emergency rooms, state and county social services agencies, plus local sheriff and police departments should be able to make a referral. Many communities have shelters for battered women. shelters provide a temporary, safe environment for women and children. They offer confidential support, advocacy, group and individual counseling and assistance with housing, child care and financial needs. These shelters are sanctuaries where women can regain a degree of self-esteem and confidence, and begin to seek resources and help for themselves and their families.

As stated earlier, drinking is often a problem for the batterer or battered, and must be addressed in order to effectively deal with the violence. Battering, combined with alcoholism, creates a most aggravated and dangerous situation. Sometimes, a temporary marital separation is necessary for the family's protection, until the drinker becomes sober. Families may find help in shelters; the alcoholic person can find help in halfway houses, or social and medical inpatient programs. (See chapter 8 regarding resources for the alcoholic.)

If separation is impossible, it is important for the victim to learn to detect signs of impending violence and physically remove herself and other possible victims from the home until it is safe to return. Sometimes, victims purposely ignore the signs of imminent violence hoping it will not happen again, thus missing their only opportunity to protect themselves from the violence. The same is true for the batterers; they, themselves, can certainly leave the premises if they perceive their own danger signs.

It is wise to be prepared for potential violence. It helps to have a plan outlining where the family can go for protection at any time of day or night. If you are the victim, it may seem strange for you to think in terms of preparing for possible violence, but the time to prepare is when you are not upset, can think clearly, and are capable of organizing reasonable protective measures. I suggest you make a list of neighbors, friends, relatives, and shelters which includes phone numbers and names. Explain to people that they may be needed for transportation, or as a refuge, and there may not be much time for advance warning. Plan ahead and pack a suitcase for such emergencies. Abusive incidents may be episodic and months may pass between incidents. Be prepared, nonetheless. If you feel you can take the risk, let the batterer know you will leave the house when you think physical abuse is a possibility. Indicate that you will return when you believe it is safe to do so. You and the batterer/alcoholic should discuss this when you are both sober and in a calm mood. Be prepared to tell the batterer you are taking this action for your own protection and for the protection of your family. Let the batterer know that when he or she becomes willing to seek help, via AA, a treatment program, therapy, etc., and you are no longer in fear of violence, you will not be forced to seek refuge. I do not suggest warning the batterer of any self-protective plans if you suspect that the response will be a violent one. If you live in a home where the battering is always precipitated by drinking, you must always approach the alcoholic when he is sober. You will have to be your own best judge as to whether to discuss your plans but you must protect yourself and your family at all costs.

SEXUAL VIOLENCE

I am apprehensive talking about this problem because I am afraid others might find out. I was seven when my dad began to touch me, and make me touch and kiss him. He did a lot of things to me, it hurt. I was 18 before it stopped, and that's because I left home then. I never told anyone. I am now only beginning to accept my past and present family situations. I withdraw from people when afraid because they know my feelings, and might hurt me. I don't visit my father and family. I just can't explain it to others. I feel guilty for never going home. I've always felt guilty.

Twenty-five million children under the age of 11 live in homes where they are sexually abused, most often by fathers or step-fathers. Incest occurs in many homes, and in all socioeconomic classes. It can be defined as inappropriate sexual behavior, usually perpetrated by an adult family member with a minor child, brought about by coercion, deception or psychological manipulation. It includes inappropriate touching, fondling, oral sex, and/or intercourse. While some victims of incest are infants, and others are in their late teens, most victims are initially approached between the ages of 5-8, with the incestuous activity usually continuing for a minimum of three years.

While research concerning incest and its relationship to alcohol abuse is limited, and varies in its conclusions, a number of studies document that over 50 percent of known incest victims lived in homes where alcohol abuse was a major problem. In addition, many private practitioners report 60 to 80 percent of the alcoholic women they treat were once incest victims. My own research indicates 26 percent of children in alcoholic homes have been incest victims. The highest incidence of incest occurs between adult fathers and young daughters, or between step-fathers and daughters. Other types of incest (mother to son, father to son, mother to daughter, extended family members to child, and sibling incest) do occur, but on considerably smaller scale. For this reason, my remarks will primarily concern the father-daughter relationship.

Consequences for Children

It is very important that incest be recognized as a reality within alcoholic families. While it is often difficult to determine the extent of the relationship between alcohol abuse and incest, it is vital to address both issues for the sake and well-being of each family member, and the generations of the family yet to come.

The effects of alcoholism coupled with incest on a young child causes serious emotional problems, both in childhood and in adulthood. Experiencing a combination of these two unhealthy life styles can be doubly traumatic for children. Many of the same unwritten rules apply equally to incest and alcoholism in the family.

The reasons children don't talk about incest are the same reasons children don't talk about alcoholism. The onset, so many times, is very gradual and children may not even recognize what is happening until the behavior has been repeated for some time. By then, children have often developed guilt feelings. The victims don't talk because of fear. . .fear that they will not be believed. "She (mom) wouldn't have believed me," or "She wouldn't have done anything about it anyway. That might have hurt more, and that would kill me," one woman responded. Another women revealed, "I do remember being really scared, like I shouldn't be doing this -- but he was my father. You listen to your father. I did it because he wanted me to do it; it was expected of me. You don't argue in my family. No one has rights in my family until you are out of the house and self-supporting."

Children are, naturally, inexperienced and vulnerable. They have no frame of reference in which they can make judgments and tend to believe anything they are told. Their own sense of confusion makes them quick to accept blame for any given situation. They naturally feel powerless in dealing with grown-ups, see themselves as unable to protect themselves, and do not perceive themselves as having available resources to protect them.

One victim explained her situation this way: "I didn't tell anybody about it. I was about eight when it started. I had a vague idea it was something bad, but I didn't know what sex was.

only knew the way he acted was something I didn't want to be part of. I would try to avoid getting into those situations. I would come home from school late hoping mom would get home first. I made up excuses not to go places alone with him. But, once it began, I just sort of passively sat there. I wouldn't talk to him, and when he let me go, I would get out of there as quickly as possible. I never told anyone what he was doing. Often times when he came into my bedroom I thought if I pretended I was asleep he would go away, and I really didn't want to acknowledge that it was happening."

Not trusting one's own feelings is experienced at an early age in an alcoholic family. The feeling is exaggerated when alcoholism is coupled with incest. Often, if the daughter in an incest relationship challenges the appropriateness of her father's sexual activity, he deceives her by saying her judgment is wrong, and his behavior is acceptable. He will often attempt to make his daughter feel guilty, and may possibly threaten her. She begins to believe her own perceptions are faulty, so will acquiesce to her father's demands. The youngster becomes intimidated and readily assumes the guilt and responsibility for her own "bad" feelings. She has learned, extremely well, how to discount her own perceptions and has developed a sense of powerlessness.

The physical act of being victimized, together with improper role modeling and nurturing, accompanied by feelings of fear, guilt and anger, lead to severe depression, and/or delinquent behaviors among young women. These victims carry emotional and psychological scars into adulthood. Many of these adult children who are sexually victimized marry men who, in turn, victimize their own children. Confusion about trust and sexuality, combined with role patterns and dynamics of NOT TALKING, NOT TRUSTING, AND NOT FEELING often cause victims to repeat these psychological dynamics in adulthood.

While many children in alcoholic homes do not experience direct sexual violation, many may, nonetheless, relate to the fear of possible sexual abuse. Others may feel an unexplainable shame about their own sexuality. A 26-year-old daughter of an alcoholic father expressed her adolescent fears to me. Even though she had never been sexually violated, she feared the possibility so much that she regularly sneaked a knife to her bedroom at night to protect herself from an anticipated attack.

This victim described her confusion as a result of the increasingly changing behavior patterns evidenced by her father. He changed from a caring, fun-loving father, to a blaming, harsh, verbally abusive, drunken stranger. This child became more fearful of her father's actions, when, along with his alcohol-induced behavior, he began talking about how "bad" it was for girls to be sexual. He became increasingly graphic in his descriptions, and began accusing the women in the family of misconduct in their sexual behavior. He demonstrated growing hostility toward the young girl's boyfriends. Eventually, he began visiting her room, late at night, to accuse her of sexual activity with boys. Her fear of possible sexual abuse by her father, coupled with the normal love a child feels for a father, led to a great sense of confusion and shame about her own sexuality. Although the father in this case did not sexually abuse the child -- she carried the emotional scars of the fear and shame she felt into her adult life.

It is obvious that adults who drink alcoholically are not proper role models for children, particularly during the time when healthy attitudes regarding sexuality need to be imparted to children. Drunken parents often speak crudely, or tease children inappropriately, with sexual innuendos. In some alcoholic homes, children are forced to deal with the drunken nudity of a parent; in other homes, parents make no attempt at maintaining discreet sex lives. The children very often face these problems, alone, in silence, confused, and feeling needless shame.

Nativity

Red hood drapes
his black robe's back
candles subdue the sanctuary,
Noel Noel we sing.

At midnight he stands before us
rolling down the words
"There was no room at the inn."
Raising his arms,
they fold down then close.

Fruitcake, poinsettias,
fudge fill our parsonage,
cookies, cards, and packages
for the minister and his family.

His daughter's presents are not wrapped.
Red tissue paper rustles, their shadows
argue against the wall
his voice commanding, "Hurry up."
He's naked swilling clear vodka.
Sobbing she cries, "You'll wake her."

Silent night
Holy night
All is calm
All is bright.

I will stay here
in this closet
until morning when
they call me
to open my presents

all the tags
in her handwriting.

                              Joan, adult child

Preventing Sexual Abuse

Be you a parent, friend or helping professional, it is mandatory for you to help young people understand they have the right to protect themselves. In working with children, or simply in normal contact with them, explain that no one has the right to touch them in certain ways, not even someone they know and love. We adults need to provide children with the psychological strength and power they need to resist unpleasant situations. Children must be allowed to say "no". They need to be free to object to behaviors which make them frightened or uncomfortable. Remember, incest often stems from an assumed perogative on the part of the offender that children are objects and possessions. The act of incest is protected by an unwritten conspiracy of silence. This coupled with the child's continuing fear and shame keeps the act hidden. Children are more likely not to be victimized when they honestly believe they are not objects, do not have to be ashamed when someone hurts them, and understand that secrets about things which make them feel bad are not to be kept. These basic messages should be communicated to all children and children should be encouraged to protect themselves against abuse. Children who know they have a right to resist and who believe another adult will support their resistance, will have a better chance of avoiding abuse by battering or incestuous parents.

Children need to hear these messages in order for them to risk applying these concepts when potentially abusive situations arise. They need to trust that they c̲a̲n̲ say "no" and have their feelings respected. We adults need to let children know we d̲o̲ take them seriously.

We need to talk with children about being "bullied" or "taken advantage of" not only by friends or brothers and sisters, but also by persons in authority, i.e. uncle, father, grandparent. In doing this, we can explain how having secrets often hurts people, and that sometimes it is not wise to keep secrets.

We need to discuss "touching" with children. We need to give them permission to not "always be nice," but to feel a sense of choice about who they touch, or who touches them. This opens up the discussion about potential sexual abuse and lets them know that should such incidents happen, they are not at fault. Then we can help them determine who should be told when such incidents occur.

Treatment

Every child who is, or has been, a victim of sexual abuse needs empathetic, professional intervention even if that intervention consists of only one visit with a social worker/helping professional. It must be made clear to children that they are not responsible for the abuse to which they have been subjected. Sexual abuse does have a tremendous impact on children. A number of variables effect the severity of a child's feeling of disruption. Among them are:
1. The personal relationship between the offender and the victim.
2. The duration of the sexual abuse.
3. The type of abuse.
4. The combination of physical and sexual abuse.
5. The child's age and stage of development.
6. The reaction of family members and other significant persons in the child's life.

Quick and responsible intervention goes a long way to alleviate the impact and lasting effects on the victim. A child alone cannot deal with the mass of questions, confusion, shame, guilt, and emotions which are a result of sexual offenses.

When incest occurs, the entire family needs help. Part of the helping process may involve reporting incest to the proper authorities, i.e. State Department of Children's Protective Services. It is likely these professional agencies can be a source of help for all the family members and may play an instrumental role in helping the courts direct the family to appropriate sources of treatment.

Adults who were child victims of incest will also benefit by counseling and therapy from a professional. Many adult victims may find solace and understanding by joining a self-help or support group comprised of other adult victims. Many times the issues of NOT TALKING, NOT TRUSTING AND NOT FEELING need to be discovered and shared by victims. Helping resources may include one-on-one therapy or group sessions.

GUIDELINES TO HELPING PROFESSIONALS

Helping professionals need to ask direct questions of clients to determine if battering or incest has occurred. Always attempt to identify whether or not alcoholism is a part of the problem. As with any sensitive issue which has been perpetuated by denial, questions should begin with the least threatening and lead up to the more concrete issues. The following is such a series of questions:

Do you and your partner argue often?

If either of you drink, are your personalities different when drinking?

Does your partner ever lose his/her temper, throw things, threaten you?

Do arguments ever end in pushing, shoving or slapping?

Has your partner ever used a fist or weapon to hurt you?

Have you ever felt the safety of your children was threatened?

The same type of questions can be asked of children, young and adult.

Does either parent ever lose their temper and slap or hit you or the other children, the furniture, the other parent?

Have you ever needed medical treatment due to an argument with a parent or sibling?

Remember, you will need to ask questions in a nonjudgmental, caring manner. As children respond, you need to be empathetic and responsive; be aware of their nonverbal messages. Again, remember, 1) they may not recognize they are/were in a battering/abusive home because of their stereotype of violent homes, 2) they have not learned the value of being able to talk 3) they have many conflicting feelings about these issues, and 4) the family members remain in physical danger if appropriate help is not obtained.

A SPECIAL MESSAGE
TO THOSE WHO WORK SPECIFICALLY WITH THE ALCOHOLIC

Do let alcoholics know you are aware of the high incidence of violence which occurs in alcoholic homes. The realization that violence is a common problem among alcoholics may make it easier for your client to admit it's part of his or her life. And be sure to ask family members about the possible abuse. Due to alcoholic blackouts, the alcoholic may honestly not remember perpetrating abusive behavior. The alcoholic has been anesthetized by the drug and he or she may not be aware of the extent of the physical or sexual violence.

But do not assume, with the onset of sobriety, that these problems will automatically cease. While alcohol usage may be associated with physical or sexual abuse, it is not always the cause. The abuse may have occurred in the alcoholic family whether or not the alcoholism was present. Remember, we know only a little about the interrelatedness between alcoholism and incest or abusive behavior. We have no way of knowing if the abusive dynamics have become a pattern now totally independent of the drinking behavior and attitude. Should the abuse cease when the drinking stops, the fears, the guilts, the angers felt by the victim do not disappear and they need to be addressed.

If you are a helping professional who is uncomfortable handling such a situation yourself, there are professional peers who are trained to work with families experiencing domestic violence. Seek out the benefit of their skills in counseling your clients. As well, all helping professionals need to be familiar with the laws of their state regarding the reporting of physical or sexual abuse. Helping professionals who are working with newly sober alcoholics may feel that they are betraying their clients in the reporting of abuse. It is important to recognize that the laws, hopefully, will be the vehicle to provide help for the abused and also for the offender. While people may suffer from the disease of alcoholism, they are still responsible for their actions.

Many times, the question is asked: "Is it detrimental to the alcoholic to bring up issues of physical violence and incest early in the recovery process?" I believe it is absolutely necessary to discuss these issues. The decision as to when to intervene varies with the circumstances, and the family and helping professionals involved should make that decision together. If the alcoholic is separated from the family, i.e. in a social or a medical treatment program, obviously the threat of violence is not imminent. However, should the alcoholic be living with the family members, this problem needs to be addressed almost immediately in order to prevent further incidents.

In a treatment setting the best time to approach the alcoholic is following detoxification and hopefully, when he or she begins to show signs of adapting to the therapeutic services offered. Again, the counselor or team of counselors, need to evaluate each individual situation. But remember not addressing violence and incest incidents does not make the issue disappear. These are issues which need to be brought out in the open so the denial and the actual acting-out end.

* * * * * *

SUMMARY

Helping professionals need to ascertain possible sexual abuse in young, adolescent and adult people, and to offer services or referrals to all those who have been victims. While it is not possible to erase the past, it is possible to diminish the unpleasant experiences of physical or psychological abuse.

As I was growing up, I remember really wanting only one thing -- to be able to do it differently than I saw it being done around me, So, when, two days before my 23rd birthday, my husband was put in jail for a felony DUI, I looked into the passive eyes of my child whom I had just thrown across the room, and felt my world and my sanity crumble. I was doing it just the same way they had done.

Two days later, I was in therapy with a psychologist who introduced me to Al-Anon and within the year I began to learn to do it differently. For the first time in my life, I began to see I had a choice. What a miraculous concept. I was building myself in to a whole person even though my husband's alcoholism progressed rapidly for the next six years.

My husband has now had five years of sobriety. We learned this is a family illness and there can be family recovery if at least one family member tries to find alternatives. I am finally doing it differently, and for me, it is a better way. At last, finally, I had a choice.

--Cindy, 34

CHAPTER 8

Resources

To Those in Need
To the Resource People

CHAPTER EIGHT

TO THOSE IN NEED

Reaching out and making that first contact with a helping resource is a big step. The act of picking up the phone, dialing the number and asking to speak to someone who can help you only takes seconds. The process which leads up to making that call for help -- the debates with yourself, the mood changes you have experienced, telling yourself you can handle the problems alone, the never-ending, continuous cycle of depression, anger, hope, guilt -- all have taken their psychological and physical toll on you and your family. So, for many, it may be months or possibly years before help is sought. But, never forget, you are worth that call.

When you begin seeking a specific resource your considerations will probably include:
1. Who are the people who will know what to do?
2. What kinds of support groups do I have available and what additional ones do I need to seek out?
3. How much can I afford to pay for help and professional services?

Making these decisions alone may seem just as overwhelming as your initial decision to seek help. But usually your own personal circumstances will quickly direct you to helping resources. With the help of a counselor or agency, you will be better able to determine the type and extent of professional help you and your family need.

Types of Help Available

The most readily available services for everyone regardless of individual circumstances are the self-help groups of Alcoholics Anonymous, Al-Anon and Alateen. These are called self-hep groups becaue they involve no professional counselors nor do they document one's involvement. They are free of charge to all who wish to participate. These groups are made up of people who identify with a common problem -- they are either alcoholic, or have a family member or friend who is alcoholic, and they are looking for a common solution -- a way of helping themselves and each other.

All of these fellowships have demonstrated themselves to be extremely helpful resources for millions of people. All provide opportunities for the child, spouse, or the alcoholic to better understand alcoholism and how it is affecting their lives. They offer every member a program of recovery, allowing each individual an avenue for feeling better about himself or herself, and helping them continue to live more productive lives. Alcoholism creates an atmosphere in which its victims and their family members become isolated and feel alone in their pain. Self-help groups offer people an opportunity to realize their experience and feelings are not unique but, in fact, that their problems are very similar to problems that each member of the group has at some time experienced. Another unifying aspect of these groups is that they practice a rule of anonymity. This means who you are is not important and, as a rule, last names are not used. In this way, no matter what your financial worth or social standing, you are considered equal with those fellow human beings who suffer from the same disease as you. Thus the groups are able to provide a sensitive non-judgmental atmosphere where the child, spouse, friend or alcoholic is able to talk about the problems being experienced and can openly express all their feelings. Each participant is helped through the support and understanding of the group, offered a simple program with guidelines to understand alcoholism and given steps to develop and sustain his or her own strengths and capabilities. AA, Al-Anon, and Alateen are also used as opportunities for social interaction and feedback from peers.

AA is a program open to any person who has a desire to stop drinking, Al-Anon members are the adult relatives or friends of someone who has a drinking problem, and Alateen is a fellowship for those between the ages of 12 and 21 who have either a family member or friend with a drinking problem. AA and Al-Anon are available throughout most towns and cities in the United States. Larger cities have meetings every day and night of the week while smaller towns may have only one or two groups per week. Unfortunately, Alateen is not as readily available as Al-Anon or AA. To contact one of these groups, simply look them up in the Yellow Pages of your local telephone directory under 'Alcoholism,' and call the Central Office of the specific group you wish to contact. They will direct you to the nearest meeting, or, if you wish, have a member contact you directly.

Depending on the community in which you live, there may be a variety of resources for the person with the drinking problem. AA is available with meetings several times a week, and often maintains a 24-hour help line. There are a variety of AA meetings, some for men only, some for women only, some for both. Some meetings offer more time for discussion, others are more for simply listening. Some are open to interested persons, while others are closed to all but alcoholics. The only requirement to become a member is the desire to stop drinking.

While Al-Anon and Alateen have been a resource for the adult spouse, friend, employer or child of an alcoholic, new groups are emerging which are focused specifically on the adult child of an alcoholic. These special groups are growing in numbers because of the understanding, energy, and positive direction other adult children derive from one another when brought together by a common problem, the alcoholism in the family. They all share a common desire to improve the quality of their lives.

Be sure to attend a number of meetings before deciding about whether or not this is an appropriate resource for you. Remember, everything feels strange and uncomfortable the first few times. Give yourself the chance to get accustomed to the group and to the varying dynamics each meeting may have to offer.

Other helpful resources listed in the Yellow Pages are special councils or centers such as the National Council on Alcoholism (NCA). Councils and Information and Referral (I&R) Centers can assist you in finding appropriate resources. Many times, these councils may provide other specific services such as crisis counseling, education and intervention services often at either no cost, or for a fee based on your ability to pay.

Unfortunately, while many resources are available for those people with drinking problems, there are not an adequate number of educational and therapy resources for the family members. Groups for both adults and children are being formed in many areas, and often these groups grow out of Al-Anon or alcoholism treatment programs. Alcoholism treatment hospitals and agencies can refer family members to helping professionals or groups. (Most treatment agencies focus predominately on alcoholics and only work with families if the alcoholic is a client or potential client.) Those agencies or private practitioners (therapists) who offer services to families affected by alcoholism are most likely to be listed in the Yellow Pages under ALCOHOLISM, PSYCHOLOGICAL SERVICES AND COUNSELING. Also, in looking for therapy resources for children, you may need to seek agencies in the mental health field i.e., child and guidance clinics and county outpatient counseling services. School counselors may also be a resource. Many times, if you ask a person in one of the helping professions (school nurse, social worker) to act as a resource, they will be most willing to do so.

Many people who have a drinking problem realize they need the assistance of a structured inpatient program to help them in the initial phase of abstinence from alcohol. Such social-based inpatient programs where the alcoholic lives at the treatment facility usually offer a short-term (two to six weeks) program offering educational sessions as well as therapy groups. Often these programs require that a person be sober for a period of twenty-four to seventy-two hours, as the program is not structured to provide detoxification services. Detoxification requires special care while the patient physically withdraws from alcohol. These programs usually have a sliding scale fee (pay what you can).

Halfway Houses may be available in your community. Halfway Houses offer long-term stays, usually from six weeks to several months, and they accommodate a small number of people (often of the same sex) who live together and follow a structured program largely based on AA principles. In these settings, the alcoholic is given peer support in maintaining sobriety and is assisted in a gradual reentry into his or her community. People who live in Halfway Houses often are helped in this effort to seek employment and sometimes provisions are made that they can continue to live there temporarily when they first start to work. Fees are normally based on ability to pay.

Many public and private hospitals have specialized detoxification services and rehabilitation programs. Because of the physical and mental complications which accompany withdrawal from alcohol and other drugs, many people may need to be in a setting where comprehensive medical services can be provided. A person is usually considered detoxified in two to seven days, depending on the amoung of alcohol consumed and their physical condition. Inpatient rehabilitation programs usually require an additional ten to thirty days treatment after detoxification. Rehabilitation consists of educational groups, therapy groups, development of support networks, individual counseling, psychological testing, family services, and aftercare planning and services. These hospital-based programs are relatively expensive, but most medical insurance will cover fifty to eighty percent (occasionally more) of the total cost.

Many times, state or county facilities have hospital-based programs for persons who lack financial assets or are without insurance. Most Veterans Administration facilities have alcoholism treatment programs.

Some alcoholism treatment agencies and county or VA services may also offer outpatient services for those who have drinking problems. Some alcoholics do not desire, or may not need, an inpatient stay. Outpatient services may be an option for people unable to be away from work, or for those without insurance or funds for inpatient programs. These programs are structured to allow the client to continue working, while attending alcohol-related groups and education classes after working hours.

Alcoholics and family members alike may be concerned if self-help or professional services are too close to home. They fear the stigma of being identified while others complain that the type of service they want seems too far away. Don't let either the fear of being "exposed" as one who has a drinking problem stop you from seeking treatment close to your home or allow the distance you must travel deter you from getting help. Be assured that whatever resource you choose confidentiality is respected and practiced. Agencies are required by law to respect confidentiality. In the same spirit AA, Al-Anon and Alateen build their programs on anonymity. For those concerned about travelling long distances to seek treatment, the hours spent in commuting to family or individual therapy sessions will be rewarded many times over the years with a happier, healthier lifestyle.

While self-help types of assistance are free of charge, mental health services offer assistance usually based on the client's ability to pay. Other services are often paid by insurance coverage. Agencies are generally able to help you determine whether or not your insurance is a reliable option. If the money for treatment must come from your pocket, remember, it may mean the saving of a life and a family. For the alcoholic, also consider the money saved when the drinking has stopped and problems are soberly addressed and resolved.

In choosing resources, options and needs will vary. Alcoholics do get sober and stay sober, and family members do get well, but first, they need to ask for help.

TO RESOURCE PEOPLE

Resource people should never underestimate the amount of difference they can make in the life of a child of an alcoholic no matter how hopeless the situation may appear. One day, at work, I received a call from a man asking if I was the woman who conducted groups for children from alcoholic homes. He explained that he had read about my work in the newspaper. When I responded that I was indeed that counselor, he told me he wanted his son, age thirteen to attend a group. He inquired about times, fees, etc. I finally was able to ask, "Who is the alcoholic in the family?" He replied, "My wife," which I expected, but then he continued, "And myself." I then asked, "Are either of you still drinking?," thinking how unlikely it would be for both to be drinking and wanting their son to participate in one of my groups "Yes, both of us," was the reply. In needing to see the parents for an "intake" it became clear that neither Derek's mother nor father would come to see me for a meeting. Finally, concerned about losing Derek completely, and aware of the difficult situation for him, I consented to have Derek be part of a group without seeing his parent first. In this situation, I knew one of two things would occur, in time, 1) One of Derek's parents would come in for help, 2) Derek wouldn't be able to return to the group. It is not likely that one member of a family, particularly the child, will continue to get well, without the other members being impacted. I was aware I could lose Derek. However, I continued to have faith that one of the parents would seek treatment, and that the time Derek spent in the group would be of value to him. After twelve weeks, my fears were realized. Derek didn't return to group. As do most helping professionals, I have faith that having been honest, sincere, warm, and offering validation and some clarification may have been enough to make life easier for this young person. I believe that the time I spent with him will enable him to reach out to another person, perhaps a relative, a neighbor, friend's parent, a counselor, a teacher; maybe someone somewhere who looks like me, or talks like me, someone else who's willing to be honest, sincere and warm. Those people do exist, and today Derek may be opening up to them just because of the few weeks that he spent where he learned to feel, to share and to trust. It may take some time before Derek is in a position to reach out, but I truly believe it will happen because this experience was a positive one.

For the Layperson

Children of alcoholics grow up never having shared their closest thoughts or feelings with even their very best friend. It is a very lonely, isolated way of growing up. This loneliness continues into adulthood because no one understood their trauma nor wanted to take the time to talk to these children.

Persons outside of an alcoholic's immediate family have a normal, and perhaps justifiable, fear of meddling in family affairs.

Problems between parents and children regarding dress codes, money, or behavior are usually resolved within the confines of the family unit. An "outsider" (even a grandparent) who takes sides invariably gets the brunt of ill feelings after the family members have reconciled these minor differences.

But, alcoholism is not a minor problem. Alcoholism is a disease which is progressive; untreated it never gets better, only worse.

Becoming a resource to the child of an alcoholic is perhaps the first step in treatment for both the child and his or her alcoholic parent. The first step in becoming that resource is to play the role of the listener -- listen, console, and help validate children's feelings. So many times, a resource person is not in a position to change the home situation, but can be a vital source in helping children withstand the pressures of the confusion in their alcoholic family. Offer guidance as it seems appropriate, but remember the best guidance can be given by qualified helping professionals knowledgeable about the disease of alcoholism.

Children are rarely aware of the availability of resources, or they feel immobilized in their own powerlessness to act on their own. A child is more likely to follow through with talking to a counselor, or to seek Alateen/Al-Anon when it is a trusted person who suggests this alternative. If possible, help in locating the specific resource. Anything one does to help bridge the connection will assist the child in getting even more help.

Children of alcoholics suffer unhealthy consequences due to lack of involvement with other people, not from concerned involvement.

Children of alcoholics come in contact with people who play a variety of roles in their lives, their parents, the extended family members, friends, neighbors, teachers, counselors, doctors, judges, etc., and each person is in a position to offer different kinds of help and support. The more these people make themselves available as knowledgeable, skilled resources, the more opportunities children of alcoholics, whether young, adolescent or adult, have to avail themselves to a wide spectrum of help. To be a viable resource, let me repeat that one must understand the problem of alcoholism and be familiar with what support systems are available to these children. If you have not had any specific education regarding alcoholism local referring agencies, self-help groups and public and private agencies are very willing to aid in your educational efforts.

To find out the availability of a specific resource for children of alcoholics, call the local National Council on Alcoholism, or the state council. Look for a listing of referral agencies under the heading of ALCOHOLISM in the Yellow Pages of the telephone directory. Call them and ask for literature.

For the Helping Professionals

Millions of children of alcoholics need the resources and skills of helping agencies and professionals. All helping professionals should address themselves to what they can do to provide answers for the problems children of alcoholics face, and determine how they can become actively involved in implementing the solutions. There is no one particular type of professional, nor any single agency, totally responsible for helping children of alcoholics. All must accept the responsibility.

Time is very precious to everyone, but if one is going to be an effective counselor, it is necessary to take extra time to better understand children of alcoholics, to talk with them, to become familiar with avenues of help and to aid them in developing additional resources.

Helping persons -- professionals, paraprofessionals and volunteers -- working in jobs where they naturally come in contact with children are prime resources for children of alcoholics. Private and public service agencies, family and child agencies, child guidance clinics, mental health agencies, youth agencies, juvenile justice systems, etc., provide wide range of services from foster care to individual and family therapy, specialized services for the physically and sexually abused, recreation services, drop-in center, Big Brother and Big Sister models. All of the people involved in such work are prime resource candidates for children of alcoholics.

Booz-Allen Hamilton, Inc. Report on Assessment of the Needs for Children of Alcoholics, 1974, summarized resources when they said: All children go to school, most families have a family doctor, and some families go to church. After the nuclear and extended family, children look, next to these general community contacts (schools, doctors and churches) for values and behavior standards and for help with their problems.

These resources are in a position to:
1. Recognize family problems when they occur.
2. Identify alcohol abuse, be in a position to refer, then support the alcoholic in treatment.
3. Provide assistance and referral for the nonalcoholic spouse.
4. Intervene and provide protection for the child, when necessary.
5. Offer moral support and encouragement and provide short-term counseling.
6. Assist the child in connecting with other needed resources.

Children must believe that a resource has something to offer, will be there, and can be counted on when needed. If a resource is patronizing, stigmatizing or ineffective, the child will not attempt to get help a second time. To become an effective resource for children of alcoholics, you must continue to learn all you can about alcoholism, how it affects the alcoholic and how the family is affected. The more one knows about alcoholism, the easier it will be to discuss difficult problems in a nonjudgmental, nonblaming manner. As you, the resource person, come to better understand alcoholism and begin to discuss it easily and openly, you will be perceived as a reliable resource and children will be more willing to take the risks of talking about their problems with you.

It is not enough merely to be aware that AA, Al-Anon, and Alateen exist. You must have an understanding of how they work. Again, attend meetings; many meetings are open to interested persons. Call the Central Offices listed in the telephone directory for information about the respective services. Be familiar with the place and time of local meetings. A resource needs to understand what AA's "12 Steps" are, and should be familiar with the idea of sponsorship. A resource should know what the "Big Book" is. You will not be a viable resource unless you are familiar with and acquire the necessary understanding to discuss these concepts. The same principles regarding attendance of meetings applies not only to those in need, but also to resource people. That is, you must attend more than one meeting in order to understand these self-help programs and how you can use this knowledge to help children of alcoholics.

While the value of self-help groups is easily apparent, unfortunately, use of Alateen by children of alcoholics is low. It is estimated that only three to five percent of children in the appropriate age group from alcoholic homes use Alateen. These children do not attend meetings for various reasons. Many times meetings are not readily available in their communities, they can't find the transportation, parents won't allow them to go, they are under the appropriate age, and perhaps the most frequent excuse -- their own denial gets in the way. "I don't need that stuff. My dad doesn't bother me. I don't bother him." Or, "They really wouldn't understand, my home situation is different. . .Not like theirs."

While some of these excuses are valid, others can be remedied. When Alateen is not available in a community, a meeting can be formed when two or more children of alcoholics band together with an adult AA and Al-Anon sponsor and begin an Alateen group. When transportation is a problem, arrangements can usually be made with other group members to share rides. Education and information are keys to overcoming those objections which discount Alateen as a resource.

Potential resources are, in fact, many times not able to perform adequately because the question of alcoholism in the family has not been identified, or if it has been identified the impact it has on the family has been discounted.

For a period of six months, I consulted by telephone with a Big Brother of a 13-year-old boy whose father was alcoholic. The Big

Brother's willingness to learn about alcoholism and his interest in understanding the youngster's denial process was vital to creating a positive and consistent role model in this youngster's life. The Big Brother was many times frustrated with the child's aloneness, unwillingness to get close and to trust. This was a Big Brother who, had he not understood the dynamics of alcoholism in the family, would probably have terminated the relationship with this youngster, creating another opportunity for the child to be rejected.

A social worker who was a caseworker in a county juvenile detention center told of how she repeatedly worked with several children from the same family because of their delinquent behavior. Physical abuse by the father was identified. Alcohol abuse was mentioned several times by the children. The children were dealt with individually, not as a family unit, and the father's treatment for alcoholism was not considered as a remedy for the physical abuse or the children's behavior. The drinking was never discussed in a manner which could have identified it as alcoholic drinking. Thus, the dynamics of alcoholism and how they contributed to the delinquent behavior of the children were left unexplored and untreated. Had this social worker been knowledgeable about alcoholism, the correct resources could have been utilized and the children helped to a healthier lifestyle.

It should be standard procedure for professionals in the helping professions to ascertain the drinking practices of the family. If the client is an adult, the drinking practices of the family during the client's childhood should also be investigated. A client, many times, will not volunteer information about alcoholism to the helping professional. This may be due to the denial system which may still persist or may be due to lack of knowledge about alcoholism. Therefore, direct questions such as the following usually lead to invalid answers: "Is there alcoholism in your family?" "Do you think one of your parents is alcoholic?" "Do you think you are an alcoholic?"

The interviewer can, many times, identify alcoholic drinking in the family by gathering information relating to drinking patterns, rather than by relying on the family member for the diagnosis. Clients and their situations differ. Each case requires a methodology of its own. The following are sample questions which when integrated into the therapy process (after some trust for the professional has been established) will lead to ascertaining the normalcy of drinking.

In asking about parental drinking:

How often does/did your mom/dad drink?

Does/did you find yourself responding differently to your parents, depending on whether or not they are drinking?

Do/did you ever get scared about your parents behavior such as drinking and driving, or violence when a parent is drinking?

Questions regarding drinking patterns:

How often do you drink?

How much do you drink?

Do you experience any problems with not remembering periods of time when you are drinking?

Has anyone, a friend, child, parent, spouse, ever commented to you about the amount you drink, or how you act when you drink?

The answers will be varied. As you increase your knowledge of the disease of alcoholism you will begin to better evaluate your client's responses and will be able to determine if the responses identify alcoholism.

Remember, a person who is alcoholic, or the spouse of the alcoholic, may also be the "child of" as well. It will be appropriate to discover if this is so, and to talk with them about alcoholism as it relates to the fact that they may always have existed in an alcoholic system.

Some helping professionals become aware of alcoholism in the home and immediately feel overwhelmed with their own powerlessness. These professionals must know that even though they may not be able to change the home situation, they can alter and positively affect how the child feels about himself. By not ignoring the information the child volunteers, the professional is saying, "You are important to me. You are of value." By active listening, by validating feelings and by making referrals, much can be accomplished in helping the child to recover. Even ten or fifteen minutes a week spent in concentrated effort can have a tremendous positive effect on a child's life. Part of the key will be in trying not to alter the family, but rather in helping the child to clarify and validate his or her own experiences. In doing this, the child of the alcoholic will be less confused and not so consumed with guilt, and will feel less anger, fear, shame, loneliness and powerlessness.

For Professionals in the School System

Schools are the resources which have the greatest access to the largest number of children. For that reason alone, they are an extremely viable resource for the identification of a child of an alcoholic. If you are a concerned teacher, counselor or administrator, you are in a position to impact children individually through direct contact, or in large numbers by impacting the school system. Teachers can recognize children who have problems at home through an assessment of their behavior --children who have problems with their school work; children who come to school sleepy or ill clad. Children who are "too good to be true" and rarely children who may speak about the subject directly. Teachers often overhear what children say to each other on the playground or in the hallways. Impressions are formed and pieces of the puzzle fit together. Often, it seems apparent that little can be done to change the home environment. But, simply being willing to listen to the children, offering them your understanding of their situation, or by simply giving solace, you can provide relief for the child in need. Offering a child validation, honesty and sincerity is offering them hope. Counselors are in a better position to discuss issues about the home directly. Principals are in a position to see that staff members are appropriately trained to be more effective resources. All staff and faculty are in a position to ask the administration for assistance in utilizing outside resources to assist in identifying these children and appropriate referral networks.

School systems need encouragement to implement curriculums

which focus on alcoholism. Such formats are being developed which allow school districts to spend anywhere from $100 to $2,500 to address children in kindergarten through twelfth grade. These programs often focus on: 1) basic education, 2) values clarification, 3) responsible decision making, and 4) self-concept. Along with many of the curriculums, connecting support systems are developed with outside agencies, (often alcoholism councils) to aid in the training and implementation of such programs. It is not as feasible for a school system to implement its own program without the assistance of training and support by the alcoholism community.

While alcohol education is a very important tool for primary prevention of future alcohol abuse, the key to its effectiveness is consistency and comprehensiveness.

The child living in the alcoholic home is more apt to identify himself or herself, once an understanding of alcoholism has been gained. Support groups for children of alcoholics are being developed and conducted by many schools across the nation. Some of the groups are peer led, others are led by community volunteers or school persons. These groups are not called therapy groups but are generally identified as rap groups, drop-in groups and support groups.

Some children living in an alcoholic home can readily be identified because the alcoholic is in a treatment facility, or because the spouse and children talk openly about the drinking. Other children are recognized as being from problematic homes due to their appearance, which indicates physical neglect, their academic performance, their poor social skills, or evident physical abuse. However, the majority of children of alcoholics are not so readily identifiable. Discussing alcoholism in a safe and nonthreatening manner will allow that child to give you some indication that alcohol is a problem in their home. When school teachers ask me how to identify children of alcoholics, I suggest they ask the question, "What do you know about alcoholism?"

An elementary education teacher in Southern California asked her class of fourth graders to draw a picture of an alcoholic. One child drew a picture and added words: "When a person has been drinking after they get off work, they come home and they say mean things to their wife and then they slap one of the kids." Obviously, this child has had first-hand experience with abusive, probably alcoholic drinking.

The child who said "An alcoholic is a bum," had only heard about the typically stereotyped skid row alcoholic. And, the child who drew a picture saying: "An alcoholic is a person who drinks so much that when they drive they often kill people," might have been exposed to an education class regarding drinking and driving, or to an alcohol awareness class depicting this consequence of drinking, (or may know of such an incident through personal experience, or through the media). Children of alcoholics will be much easier to identify when we talk more openly about alcoholism, look for the signs of the effects of alcoholism in the children and then listen to what they have to say.

For Professionals in The Alcoholism Field

In addition to self-help groups, alcoholism treatment programs are in an excellent position to offer professional resources for children of alcoholics. While the primary goal of all alcoholism treatment programs is the achievement and maintenance of sobriety for the alcoholic, these programs recognize, and are beginning to develop, services for the alcoholics entire family. In the past 10 years, treatment facilities have particularly escalated services to address the spouse. Much of the work enables the spouse to better understand both the alcoholic and the disease process with more effort now being directed to help the spouse understand his or her own co-alcoholism. Most programs have not yet expanded services to address the young, adolescent or adult child. It is vital that specific groups be developed in educational and therapy modes and that the groups focus on the family disease process. It is also important that such therapy be offered to all family members. Young, adolescent and adult children need information and therapy provided in a safe environment --an environment in which they can learn about the disease process and, ultimately, receive help for themselves. Children need to be addressed separately from their parents. They must be able to effectively focus on their own guilt, anger, fear, lonliness and denial without the stifling influence of a parent's presence.

By the time many alcoholics seek help, their children are adults. These, now adult, children must also play an active role in the family recovery program. Through their participation, these adult children will come to have a better understanding of themselves and, hopefully, lead happier, fuller lives. In my work with inpatient alcoholic treatment programs, I strongly encouraged, no, demanded, that the adult child be a part of the family recovery program. I met with each child, individually, and had them share their situations, problems and lives with me. I believe if they had not been involved in a therapeutic process, they would have little understanding about themselves, and would continue to live their lives NOT TALKING, NOT FEELING AND NOT TRUSTING, but merely surviving in lives filled with voids and gaps. Many times, such a treatment program is the turning point in the lives of children of alcoholics; not only might their parents get sober and stay sober, but wonderfully, the children themselves may begin their own recovery process.

* * * * * *

SUMMARY

It is of paramount importance that resources for children do not underestimate the impact they have on a child, no matter how limited in power or time resources perceive themselves to be. I believe very few helping professionals will ever have all the ideal means -- the staff, space, money or time -- necessary to develop the number of comprehensive services desired. But if each assesses what can be done with the means at hand, they can actualize resources on the spot. With even a little greater effort, intermediate and long range goals can be developed. To say we "just can't do it all' is delinquent behavior on our part, which really says "we don't care enough." Everyone can do slightly

more than they are doing right now. Doing slightly more means
possibly:

- talking with a family member
- being willing to talk to a daughter's friend
- asking the board you sit on to address the issue
- asking a clergy person to address this issue with peers, or in a "family group"
- asking a doctor to see the children when alcoholism is identified in the adult
- expanding questions in intake procedures to better ascertain possible alcoholism
- discussing alcoholism when identified
- referring to appropriate treatment when necessary
- developing specific treatment for children of alcoholics
- expanding individual and group services to this specific client population

These actions take a willingness to become involved, a willingness to help improve the quality of someone else's life

Children of alcoholics will be adequately addressed and helped only when we, lay people and professionals alike, all begin to take responsibility. Everyone who has access to the child needs to take some responsibility. Resources also need to be supportive to each other. Keep in mind, some programs are structured in such a way that they can do little work with children, other programs may be able to work more extensively with children, but all programs have access to either the young, adolescent or adult child from many alcoholic homes. If you are willing to ask yourself what help you can provide within the structure of your program, then, you are taking the first step.

I FEEL LIKE IVE BEEN ON A ROLLACOASTER
FOR A REAL LONG TIME. I WANT OFF.

Janice 44

EPILOGUE

Shortly after I began It Will Never Happen to Me I also initiated an original and extensive research project related to children of alcoholics. In this research I am attempting to establish new facts and to clarify existing information. I am hoping to ascertain possible predicting variables that may influence one child versus another to become alcoholic, or to marry an alcoholic. I wanted more knowledge regarding why it is that some children do not continue to become alcoholic, or marry an alcoholic, and if they do not, are there identifiable primary problem areas for the specific child. I proceeded to acquire information from a sample group of over four hundred adult children of alcoholics and established a control group (sample of people not raised in alcoholic homes) so that I might compare the data.

While I have been seeking to obtain information that I believe will be of great interest to the reader I have not incorporated this data into the book (other than for spartan excerpts in the family violence chapter) as the research is not yet complete. Yet there are a few items that I think are of interest that I would like to share.

As I suspected, my research indicates that children are not more likely to become alcoholic when mom is alcoholic versus dad. Some professionals say that considering the greater amount of time that children spend with their mothers rather than fathers that they would be more severely affected. However, when the sex of the alcoholic parent was singled out that statement did not prove to be true. Research indicated that aside from the sex of the alcoholic parent other variables have greater predicting factors.

While I was aware of the tendency of daughters to marry alcoholic men I was surprised to see that sons of alcoholic parents marry women who become (or are) alcoholics and with the same frequency.

In asking about role identification nearly all respondents identified with not one role but a combination of at least two roles. Over 63% of the sample saw themselves as very sensitive young people, often placating; they combined that placating role with being responsible or combined their extreme sensitivity with problematic behavior. Sixty percent saw themselves as very mature young people, identifying themselves with being responsible. Forty-three percent said they had excellent adjusting abilities. Problematic children were in the minority with only 21% of the group identifying with such behavior.

I am finding this research most exciting. I believe it will offer all of us more specific information. I hope to begin publication of this data in the near future.

As I was working on the research and It Will Never Happen To Me I have continued to provide training seminars across the nation. I am very pleased with the increasing interest and concern for children of alcoholics and the growing number of resources available to them. Private therapists are asking for more information, identifying alcoholics in the family and working with the appropriate issues. Clergypeople and physicians are talking to their congregations and clients more openly and directly. Schools are more willing and less fearful to identify a role they can play and the alcoholism field is expanding their concept of family to mean more than 'spouse'. There is much more information to be generated and resources to be developed but the process has begun. Children of alcoholics are an identifiable group with special needs who can be addressed, will be addressed and are being helped.

APPENDIXES

APPENDIX A

C.A.S.T

C.A.S.T can be used to identify latency age, adolescent, and grown up children of alcoholics.

Please check (✓) the answer below that best describes your feelings, behavior, and experiences related to a parent's alcohol use. Take your time and be as accurate as possible. Answer all 30 questions by checking either "yes" or "no."

Sex: Male____   Female____   Age:____

Yes	No	Questions
____	____	1. Have you ever thought that one of your parents had a drinking problem?
____	____	2. Have you ever lost sleep because of a parent's drinking?
____	____	3. Did you ever encourage one of your parents to quit drinking?
____	____	4. Did you ever feel alone, scared, nervous, angry, or frustrated because a parent was not able to stop drinking?
____	____	5. Did you ever argue or fight with a parent when he or she was drinking?
____	____	6. Did you ever threaten to run away from home because of a parent's drinking?
____	____	7. Has a parent ever yelled at or hit you or other family members when drinking?
____	____	8. Have you ever heard your parents fight when one of them was drunk?
____	____	9. Did you ever protect another family member from a parent who was drinking?
____	____	10. Did you ever feel like hiding or emptying a parent's bottle of liquor?
____	____	11. Do many of your thoughts revolve around a problem drinking parent or difficulties that arise because of his or her drinking?
____	____	12. Did you ever wish that a parent would stop drinking?
____	____	13. Did you ever feel responsible for and guilty about a parent's drinking.
____	____	14. Did you ever fear that your parents would get divorced due to alcohol misuse?
____	____	15. Have you ever withdrawn from and avoided outside activities and friends because of embarassment and shame over a parent's drinking problem?
____	____	16. Did you ever feel caught in the middle of an argument or fight between a problem drinking parent and your other parent?
____	____	17. Did you ever feel that you made a parent drink alcohol?
____	____	18. Have you ever felt that a problem drinking parent did not really love you?
____	____	19. Did you ever resent a parent's drinking?
____	____	20. Have you ever worried about a parent's health because of his or her alcohol use?
____	____	21. Have you ever been blamed for a parent's drinking?
____	____	22. Did you ever think your father was an alcoholic?

APPENDIX A (continued)

____ ____ 23. Did you ever wish your home could be more like the homes of your friends who did not have a parent with a drinking problem?

____ ____ 24. Did a parent ever make promises to you that he or she did not keep because of drinking?

____ ____ 25. Did you ever think your mother was an alcoholic?

____ ____ 26. Did you ever wish that you could talk to someone who could understand and help the alcohol-related problems in your family?

____ ____ 27. Did you ever fight with your brothers and sisters about a parent's drinking?

____ ____ 28. Did you ever stay away from home to avoid the drinking parent or your other parent's reaction to the drinking?

____ ____ 29. Have you ever felt sick, cried, or had a "knot" in your stomach after worrying about a parent's drinking?

____ ____ 30. Did you ever take over any chores and duties at home that were usually done by a parent before he or she developed a drinking problem?

____ **TOTAL NUMBER OF "YES" ANSWERS.**

Score of 6 or more means that more than likely this child is child of an alcoholic parent.

© **1982 by John W. Jones, Ph.D. Family Recovery Press.**

APPENDIX B

Are You An Alcoholic?

To answer this question ask yourself the following questions and answer them as honestly as you can.

	Yes	No
1. Do you lose time from work due to drinking?	☐	☐
2. Is drinking making your home life unhappy?	☐	☐
3. Do you drink because you are shy with other people?	☐	☐
4. Is drinking affecting your reputation?	☐	☐
5. Have you ever felt remorse after drinking?	☐	☐
6. Have you gotten into financial difficulties as a result of drinking?	☐	☐
7. Do you turn to lower companions and an inferior environment when drinking?	☐	☐
8. Does your drinking make you careless of your family's welfare?	☐	☐
9. Has your ambition decreased since drinking?	☐	☐
10. Do you crave a drink at a definite time daily?	☐	☐
11. Do you want a drink the next morning?	☐	☐
12. Does drinking cause you to have difficulty in sleeping?	☐	☐
13. Has your efficiency decreased since drinking?	☐	☐
14. Is drinking jeopardizing your job or business?	☐	☐
15. Do you drink to escape from worries or trouble?	☐	☐
16. Do you drink alone?	☐	☐
17. Have you ever had a complete loss of memory as a result of drinking?	☐	☐
18. Has your physician ever treated you for drinking?	☐	☐
19. Do you drink to build up your self-confidence?	☐	☐
20. Have you ever been to a hospital or institution on account on drinking?	☐	☐

If you have answered YES to any one of the questions, there is a definite warning that **You may be alcoholic.**

If you have answered YES to any two, the chances are that you **are an alcoholic.**

If you have answered YES to **three or more, you are definitely an alcoholic.**

(The above Test Questions are used by John Hopkins University Hospital, Baltimore, Md., in deciding whether or not a patient is alcoholic.)

DATE DUE